Women
in Islam

Margaret Speaker Yuan, *Book Editor*

Bruce Glassman, *Vice President*
Bonnie Szumski, *Publisher*
Helen Cothran, *Managing Editor*

GREENHAVEN PRESS
An imprint of Thomson Gale, a part of The Thomson Corporation

Detroit • New York • San Francisco • San Diego • New Haven, Conn.
Waterville, Maine • London • Munich

THOMSON

GALE

LIBRARY OF CONGRESS CATALOGING-IN-PUBLICATION DATA

Women in Islam / Margaret Speaker Yuan, book editor.
    p. cm. — (At issue)
    Includes bibliographical references and index.
    ISBN 0-7377-2759-4 (lib. : alk. paper) — ISBN 0-7377-2760-8 (pbk. : alk. paper)
    1. Women in Islam. 2. Muslim women—Social conditions. 3. Muslim women—Islamic countries—Social conditions. I. Speaker Yuan, Margaret. II. At issue (San Diego, Calif.)
    BP173.4.W69 2005
    297'.092—dc22   2004054104

Printed in the United States of America

Contents

Introduction

Much of the debate about women's status in Islam centers on interpretations of the Koran (Islam's sacred text), the hadith (commentaries on the Koran), and the sharia (Islamic legal codes). Until the last century the sections of these texts that could have been used to support greater rights for women were suppressed. Instead, the portions that restricted woman's rights were widely taught, even when their authorship and authority were questionable. Furthermore, because women did not have the right to an education and few women could read, women were unable to interpret the texts for themselves. As a result patriarchal, discriminatory interpretations based exclusively on men's opinions were the norm. For centuries after the prophet Muhammad's death in the seventh century, women were widely considered inferior to men. Intellectually and physically, women were seen as the weaker sex. By both law and custom, women faced discrimination in all areas of life.

Today Islamic women are increasingly questioning interpretations of the Koran, the hadith, and the sharia that give men dominant positions over women. Yet there is no consensus, even among contemporary Islamic scholars, on what women's roles should be. Three main schools of thought about the women's role in Islam have developed. These are the traditionalist, the feminist, and the progressive.

The traditionalist view: Islam liberates women

Traditionalists believe that all women are inferior to any man. In their view the Islamic texts teach that women are happier and society is stronger when women obey men's decisions in all aspects of life. Traditionalists hold that their view of women is natural and biologically determined by sexual differences. As Abdul-Hakim Murad, a British convert to Islam and a Koranic scholar, says in his essay *Boys Will Be Boys*, "an opposition to the Shari'a is an opposition to science, inasmuch as science is currently affirming an innate distinction between the sexes, a distinction that Allah clearly calls us to celebrate rather than to

5

suppress." In this view women have many rights under traditional Islam that are more important than mere equality.

One of the most important of these rights is that of full financial support for wives and children. Traditionalists believe that all women, without exception, desire children and can only become happy and fulfilled as mothers. They also say that because of their inferior intellect and physical weakness, women cannot compete with men in the workplace. As conservative scholar Yusuf Al Qaradawy writes in his book *The Status of Women in Islam,*

> When the woman is involved in men's work without restrictions or limits it has its harmful effect on various aspects. It is harmful on social life because going against the grains of nature and dislocating things which are naturally located . . . [it] spoils life itself and causes imbalance, disorder, and chaos.

No examination of the traditionalist view of the women's position in Islamic societies would be complete without considering Islamic clothing. Although the Koran instructs both men and women to be modest in their attire, only women in Islamic societies are required to wear specific types of Islamic clothing, which vary from the *hijab* (the Islamic headscarf) to the burka (a full-length garment that covers the entire body including the eyes). Traditionalists see this Islamic dress as liberating for women, as it shows their piety and frees them from being judged by appearance.

To summarize, traditionalists believe that women are liberated by fulfilling their biological destiny as mothers, by devoting themselves to housekeeping, by receiving financial support from their husbands, and by wearing Islamic clothing. Women and men have clearly defined roles in separate spheres that fulfill the natural proclivities of both sexes, thus liberating both men and women from the oppression of unwanted roles or activities.

The feminist view: Islam oppresses women

Feminists hold that the so-called rights granted to women by traditional Islam in fact reflect a biased and unsound view of both women and men. The roles that traditional Islam assigns to women are seen as repressive barriers to freedom that keep women in subjugation. They also argue that the traditional Islamic view that women are weak and intellectually inferior leads inevitably to their oppression. To end this oppression, feminists favor complete secularization of Islamic societies and equal legal rights for women.

One of the most oppressive aspects of traditional Islam, according to feminists, is the denial of women's marital and reproductive rights. Women do not have the right to decide whom to marry, when to have sexual relations, or whether to use contraception. Women do not have any control over whether their husbands decide to marry additional wives. Women cannot initiate divorce, nor do they have any recourse against being divorced. As Islamic scholar Kecia Ali writes in her essay "Progressive Muslims and Islamic Jurisprudence," "This [marriage] system was predicated, at a very basic logical level, on an analogy to slavery and other types of ownership."

Another aspect of traditional Islam that feminists view as oppressive is the clothing women are required to wear. They believe that it is completely dehumanizing. Clothing that covers the hair, the body, and the face denies women individuality. Since men are not required to cover themselves, women should not be forced into uncomfortable clothing that makes one woman indistinguishable from another, they argue.

Feminists do not believe that this oppression of Islamic women will end until Islamic countries cease to base their government and laws on the sharia and Islamic customs. In their view women will only achieve equality under a secular government. For feminist writers such as Azam Kamguian, Islam is inimical to women's rights. She writes, "Attempting to modernize or reform Islam will only prolong the age-old subordination of women in Islam-stricken societies. Rather than modernizing Islam, it must be caged."

The progressive view: Islamic framework needed for woman's rights

Whereas feminists believe that women will never achieve equality under the laws of Islam, progressives argue that Islam is not inherently biased against women. While they do believe that the Koran is the revealed word of God that must be read and studied by all worshippers, they do not accept the authority of centuries-old interpretations of the prophet's words that argue that women are weak and inferior. Progressive Muslims believe that their own interpretations of the sacred texts are as valid as those of any previous scholars.

Women studying the Koran have found omissions in some published texts that change the interpretation of many verses. Acting on their own evaluations of the Koran, progressive Muslims claim the right to decide whether to work, to wear Islamic clothing, or to have children. Progressives demand the right to make choices as informed, intelligent human beings. Obedience to God, for progressives, is not the same thing as obedience to men. God guides women's choices in the same way that God guides men's choices. As Zainah Anwar, the executive director of Sisters in Islam, writes in *Beyond the Veil*, "More than ever, there is a need for Muslims to differentiate between what is divine and what is human—the source of the law is divine, but the human effort in understanding God's message, the human effort in codifying God's message into positive law, is not infallible and divine."

One of the clearest examples of progressive Islamic thought concerns clothing. Many progressive Islamic women choose to wear Islamic dress as an expression of their piety and modesty. For progressives, forcing women to wear the veil is as oppressive as forcing them to unveil. They regard the choice of clothing as a personal one, dictated by one's readings of the sacred text.

The debate over women's status in Islam will continue to be controversial, as it concerns some of the most important aspects of life and society, including marital relationships, economic equality, and the freedom and rights of women. A diversity of viewpoints ranging from traditionalist to feminist to progressive are represented in *At Issue: Women in Islam.* Understanding these viewpoints will lead to a clearer understanding of Islam.

1

The Koran Teaches That Women Have the Same Rights as Men

Amina Wadud

Amina Wadud is an associate professor of Islamic studies in the Department of Philosophy and Religious Studies at Virginia Commonwealth University. She is the author of Qur'an and Woman: Rereading the Sacred Text from a Woman's Perspective.

According to the Koran, women and men were created as equals. Both sexes have rights to inheritance, independent property, and divorce as well as the right to testify in a court of law. However, after the death of the prophet Muhammad, male leaders began to move away from the Koran's ethical codes for female autonomy and instead advocate women's subservience to men. Women scholars today read and interpret sacred texts for themselves and are challenging the patriarchal interpretations that have held them in bondage for centuries. Women are also working for legal reforms so that they can participate at all levels of society.

I converted to Islam during the second wave feminist movement in the 1970s. I saw everything through a prism of religious euphoria and idealism. Within the Islamic system of thought I have struggled to transform idealism into pragmatic reforms as a scholar and activist. And my main source of inspiration has been Islam's own primary source—the Qur'an.

It is clear to me that the Qur'an aimed to erase all notions of women as subhuman. There are more passages that address issues relating to women—as individuals, in the family, as members of the community—than all other social issues combined.

Qur'anic story of human origins

Let's start with the Qur'anic story of human origins. 'Man' is not made in the image of God. Neither is a flawed female helpmate extracted from him as an afterthought or utility. Dualism is the primordial design for all creation: 'From all (created) things are pairs' (Qur'an, chapter 51, verse 49).

Therefore, when the proto-human soul, self or person (*nafs*) is brought into existence, its mate (*zawj*) is already a part of the plan. The two dwell in a state of bliss: the Garden of Eden. They are warned against Satan's temptation but they forget and eat from the tree. When the Qur'an recounts the event in the Garden, it uses the unique dual form in Arabic grammar showing that both were guilty. The female is never singled out and chastised for being a temptress.

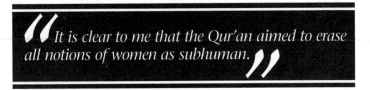

It is clear to me that the Qur'an aimed to erase all notions of women as subhuman.

Ultimately, the two seek forgiveness and it is granted. They begin life on earth untainted by a 'fall' from grace and with no trace of original sin. On the contrary, in Islam the creation story for humans on earth begins with forgiveness and mercy as well as a most important promise or covenant from God. He/She/It will provide guidance through revelation. Adam is the first prophet.

Furthermore, the Qur'an is emphatic that since Allah is not created then He/She/It cannot be subject to or limited by created characteristics, like gender. That Arabic grammar carries gender markers has led even the best Arab grammarians erroneously to attribute gender to the thing referred to. Modern feminist studies have analyzed this gender bias in language.

Changes brought by Islam

Islam brought radical changes regarding women and society, despite the deeply entrenched patriarchy of seventh-century

Arabia. The Qur'an provides women with explicit rights to inheritance, independent property, divorce and the right to testify in a court of law. It prohibits wanton violence towards women and girls and is against duress in marriage and community affairs. Women and men equally are required to fulfill all religious duties, and are equally eligible for punishment for misdemeanors. Finally, women are offered the ultimate boon: paradise and proximity to Allah: 'Whoever does an atom's weight of good, whether male or female, and is a believer, all such shall enter into Paradise' (Qur'an, chapter 40, verse 40).

> *The Qur'an provides women with explicit rights to inheritance, independent property, divorce and the right to testify in a court of law.*

In the period immediately following the death of the Prophet, women were active participants at all levels of community affairs—religious, political, social, educational, intellectual. They played key roles in preserving traditions, disseminating knowledge and challenging authority when it went against their understanding of the Qur'an or the prophetic legacy.

The Prophet's favorite wife A'ishah, from whom the Prophet said we should learn 'half our religion', was sought after as an advisor to the early jurists. In the famous 'Battle of the Camel' she was an army general. The Prophet even received revelation while resting his head on her lap. Unfortunately, this period passed before it could establish a pattern sustainable as historical precedent. And the name of A'ishah cannot erase what was to happen to the status of women in the following thousand years.

Male leaders began to ignore Islam's ethical codes

During the Abbasid period, when Islam's foundations were developed, leading scholars and thinkers were exclusively male. They had no experience with revelation first hand, had not known the Prophet directly and were sometimes influenced by intellectual and moral cultures antithetical to Islam.

In particular, they moved away from the Qur'an's ethical

codes for female autonomy to advocate instead women's sub-servience, silence and seclusion. If women's agency was taken into consideration it was with regard to service to men, family and community. Women came to be discussed in law in the same terms as material objects and possessions. (This is today reflected in Pakistan's rape laws which treat the offense as one of theft of male private property with no consideration for the woman's rights).

Not until the post-colonial 20th century would Muslim women re-emerge as active participants in all areas of Islamic public, political, economic, intellectual, social, cultural and spiritual affairs.

Muslim women today

Today Muslim women are striving for greater inclusiveness in many diverse ways, not all of them in agreement with each other. At the Beijing Global Women's Conference in 1995, nightly attempts to form a Muslim women's caucus at the non-governmental organization (NGO) forum became screaming sessions. The many different strategies and perspectives just could not be brought to a consensus. On the Left were many secular feminists and activists who, while Muslim themselves, defined Islam on a cultural basis only. Their politics was in-formed by post-colonialist and Marxist agendas of nationalism. Concrete issues of women's full equality: standards of educa-tion, career opportunities, political participation and represen-tation were understood in Western terms. The cultural imposi-tion of veiling was to them a symbol of women's backwardness; for them full entry in the public domain and other indicators of liberation were reflected in Western styles of dress.

On the far Right, Muslim male authorities and their female representatives, known as Islamists, spearheaded a reactionary, neo-conservative approach. They identified an ideal Islam as the one lived by the Prophet's companions and followers at Madinah. All that was required today was to lift that ideal out of the pages of history and graft it on to modernity adopting a complete *shari'ah* [Islamic law] state, unexamined and unques-tioned and opposed to modern complexity. Then life would be perfect. There were no inequities towards women because the law was divine and the matter of patriarchal interpretation was irrelevant. Female Islamists representing this viewpoint handed out booklets (written by men) with titles such as 'The Wisdom behind Islam's Position on Women'. Although the arguments were not intellectually rigorous or critically substantial they held a substantial sway. Ironically, these arguments would also form part of the rhetoric used by secular feminists to discredit human-rights and social-justice advocates who were in the middle ground, who insisted on fighting from within an Islamic perspective, or who happen to wear *hijab* [Islamic dress, specifically the head scarf].

As the term 'Islamic feminism' gained currency in the 1990s through scholars and activists, it would clarify the perspective of a large number of women somewhere between Islamists and secular feminists. While they would not give up their allegiance to Islam as an essential part of self-determination and identity they did critique patriarchal control over the basic Islamic world-view. Islamic feminism did not define these women, and many still reject the term. However, the term helped others to understand the distinction between them and the two dominant approaches for Muslim women's rights.

Today more women are active in the discussion and reformation of identity than at any other time in human history. By going back to primary sources and interpreting them afresh, women scholars are endeavoring to remove the fetters imposed by centuries of patriarchal interpretation and practice. By questioning underlying presumptions and conclusions they are creating a space in which to think about gender. Drawing upon enduring principles of human rights, enshrined in the text, they extract meanings that can interact with the changing moral and intellectual circumstances of the reader. And women scholars and activists are also busy constructing a system of legal reforms that can be implemented today for the full status of women as moral agents at all levels of human society.

This moral agency is a mandate of the Qur'an and cannot be restricted by any amount of historical precedent, social custom or patriarchal aspiration. The long-term success of this project lies in the fact that it is all happening within Islam. And the rationale for change comes from the most trustworthy and reliable source of Islam itself—the Qur'an.

2

The Koran Teaches That Women Do Not Have the Same Rights as Men

Azam Kamguian

Azam Kamguian is an Iranian writer and woman's rights activist. She is the founder and the chairperson of the Committee to Defend Women's Rights in the Middle East and editor of its bulletin Women in the Middle East. *Azam's numerous articles on women, religion, Islam, and social issues have been published in various Persian and international newspapers and journals. She has also appeared on TV and radio programs around the world. Her books include* Islam, Women, Challenges and Perspectives; Feminism; Socialism and Human Nature; On Religion; Women's Liberation and Political Processes in the Middle East; Islam and Women's Rights; Iranian Women's Movement for Equality; *and* Godlessness, Freedom from Religion and Human Happiness.

Verses from the Koran show overwhelmingly that women's status in Islam has always been inferior to men's status. Women are seen as weak, perpetually immature, and incapable of independent thought. They cannot leave their houses or travel without a male guardian. All decisions about a woman's personal life, including when to have sexual relations, are made by men. Only through resistance to Islam will women gain equality and human rights.

Religion in general and Islam in particular are women's enemy. Women's inequality is god's commandment, in Islam enshrined in immutable law by Mohammad and eventually recorded in scripture. In most countries under Islamic states or under the influence of Islam, Koran's directives are incorporated into contemporary law.

Family law in these countries generally follows the prescriptions of Koran. Veiling (hijab), divorce laws, a very young legal age of marriage, custody of children, polygamy, women's rightlessness in matters of employment, travelling, choosing the place of residence, honour killing are all aspects of Islamic Shari'a [law] based on the Koran and Islam's doctrine. Together with these, in countries under the Islamic states, women are stoned to death for engaging in voluntary sexual relations and are stripped of their basic human rights.

As many Western and Eastern apologists for Islam repeatedly tell us that what is happening to women in the so-called Islamic countries is not according to real Islam, and that real Islam is egalitarian, I mainly refer to the Koran. Laws about women are the most cruel, inhumane and cunning aspects of the Koran and Islamic Shari'a.

Women as the inferior sex

The rigid laws of Islam have deprived half of the population of their basic human rights. The male is in charge of the female: Koran 4:34, and the subjugated half is led to believe, through Islamic teachings, that the supremacy of the man is the will of Allah, and it has been predestined for women to live as submissive, obedient wives. They are forced to accept that women are inferior to men, that their testimony is equal to only half that of the man, that they should inherit one-half of the male share, that Allah doesn't want to see any women unveiled, that she may not converse with men except her father, or her brother. The proper job and position for women is taking care of home, children and to be a housewife. The majority of Muslim women are brought up with the conviction that it is Allah's command for them to be under male dominance and their fates are interwoven with that of men.

In the Koran there are four so-called neutral verses where women are considered equal to men (at least not demeaning towards women); to which apologists for Islam refer us repeatedly. Here are those:

3:195 "Their Lord responded to the: "I never fail to reward any worker among you for any work you do, be you male or female, you are equal to one another."

4:124 "As for those who lead a righteous life, male or female. While believing, they enter paradise; without the slightest injustice."

16:97 "Anyone who works righteousness, male or female, while believing, we will surely grant them a happy life in this world, and we will surely pay them their full recompense for their righteous works."

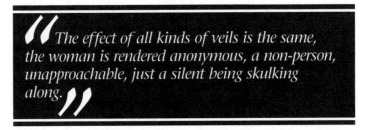

The effect of all kinds of veils is the same, the woman is rendered anonymous, a non-person, unapproachable, just a silent being skulking along.

40:40 "Whoever commits a sin is required for just that, and whoever works righteousness—male or female—while believing, these will enter paradise wherein they receive provision without any limits."

In opposition to the above four so-called neutral verses, there are hundreds of verses that deliberately defame and dehumanise women:

An-Nisa 4:34 "As to those women On whose part ye fear disloyalty and ill-conduct, admonish them (first), (next) refuse to share beds, (and last) beat them (lightly); but if they return to obedience, seek not against them means (of annoyance): For God is Most High, Great (above you all)."

Al-Baqara 2:223 "Your women are a tilt for you (to cultivate) so go to your tilt as ye will, and send (good deeds) before you for your souls, and fear Allah, and know that ye will (one day) meet Him. Give glad tidings to believers, (O Mohammad)."

Al-Baqara 2:222 "They questioned thee (O Mohammad) concerning menstruation, Say it is an illness, so let women alone at such times and go not unto them till they are cleansed."

Al-Baqara 2:228 "Men, your wives are your tillage. Go into your tillage any way you want."

"Women have such honourable rights as obligations, but men have a (single) degree above them."

"Men are managers of the affairs of women because Allah has preferred men over women and women were expended of their rights."

4:6 "And if ye are sick on a journey, or one of you cometh from the closet, or ye have contact with a woman & ye find not water, then go to clean high ground & rub your faces & your hands with some of it."

33:32–33 "O ye wives of the prophet! Ye are not like any other women. If ye keep your duty (to Allah), then be not soft of speech lest he in whose heart is a disease aspire to you, but utter customary speech And stay in your houses. Bedizen not yourselves with the bedizenment of the time of ignorance. Be regular in prayer, and pay the poor due, and obey Allah and His messenger."

Women's moral inferiority

[Further citations from the Koran] "If a man and woman are alone in one place, the third person present is the devil."

"I was shown the hell-fire and that the majority of its dwellers were women who were ungrateful."

"If it had been given me to order someone to prostrate themselves in front of someone other than God, I would surely have ordered women to prostrate themselves in front of their husbands."

"A woman cannot fulfil her duties towards god without first having accomplished those that she owes her husband."

"The woman who dies and with whom the husband is satisfied will go to paradise."

"A wife should never refuse herself to her husband even if it is on the saddle of a camel."

"Hellfire appeared to me in a dream and I noticed that it was above all people with women who had been ungrateful. "Was it towards god that they were ungrateful?" They had not shown any gratitude towards their husbands for all they had received from them. Even when all your life you have showered a woman with your largesse she will still find something petty to reproach you with one day, saying, "You have never done anything for me."

"If anything presages a bad omen it is a house, a woman, and a horse."

"Never will a people know success if they confide their affairs to a woman."

One of the most misogynist Islamic laws with respect to women is the requirement for complete veiling (hijab) in accordance with Koranic tenets. The wearing of the veil was instituted by Mohammad in the early days of Islam. Within about one hundred years of his death, the institution of veiling and seclusion had been spread all over the Middle East. One and a half centuries after his death, the system was fully established.

The effect of all kinds of veils is the same, the woman is rendered anonymous, a non-person, unapproachable, just a silent being skulking along. She is taboo. The Islamic head-cover mentioned in Koran 33: 59, and the curtain referred to in Koran 33: 53, which was meant to separate the man from the woman. Why is Islam so obsessed with keeping men and women part? Why have Islam gone to such great lengths to maintain control over women?

The main reason for hijab is the need for controlling women's sexuality. Veiling internalises the Islamic notion in women that they belong to an inferior sex, and that they are sex objects. It teaches them to limit their physical movements and their free behaviour. Veiling is a powerful tool to institutionalise women's segregation and to implement a system of sexual apartheid. It signifies the subjugation and servitude of women based on Islamic doctrine and Koranic teachings. Much more than a way of clothing, hijab is the manifestation of an outright Islamic misogynism and an antiquated view on women's status. It is designed to control women's sexuality much more effectively than any other religion or ideological system.

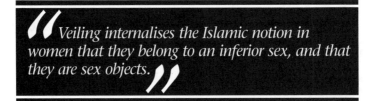

Veiling internalises the Islamic notion in women that they belong to an inferior sex, and that they are sex objects.

The following quote is attributed to Mohammad by a number of Hadith [scripture] collectors: "A woman is a pudendum (awrat) which is proper to hide and cover; therefore when a woman goes out Satan looks at her and desire to carry her from the road." In the eyes of Mohammad, according to this quote, all male believers are potential "Satans" who might try to take unconcealed women for themselves.

Mohammad himself was one of the men who were unable to control their lust upon looking at women. Once he visited the home of Zayd, his adopted son, and there saw Zaynab, Zayd's wife, half-naked. Mohammad's obvious desire for the woman eventually led to the divorce of Zayd from his wife and shortly thereafter Mohammad married her himself.

The law of veiling is not only humiliating to women, but it is an insult to men. It is a clear indication that, in the eyes of Mohammad; all Muslim males were sex-crazed. The obvious implication is that seeing a woman without a veil would cause the typical Muslim male to lose control and that unveiled women would constantly be subjected to unwanted sexual advances.

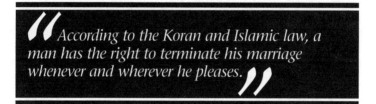

According to the Koran and Islamic law, a man has the right to terminate his marriage whenever and wherever he pleases.

Veil (hijab) is imposed on women in many countries under the influence of Islam, either legally or under cultural and social pressure. During the last thirty years, hijab has been and continues to be the political and ideological symbol of political Islam, Islamic states and the Islamic movement in the Middle East, North Africa and Central Asia. Women have been the first-hand victims of this reactionary movement, and imposing the veil on women by Islamic movement and Islamic governments has been their first bloody action to suppress the whole society. In other countries, Saudi women typically don a billowy black cloak called an Abaya, along with a black scarf and veil over the face. Morality police enforce the dress code by striking errant women with sticks. The women of Iran and the Sudan can expose the face, but should cover the hair and the neck. Otherwise they face arrest, imprisonment, flogging, cash fines; and if they refuse it, they face knife and acid attack. Under Taliban [former Afghanistan fundamentalist ruling party], women of Afghanistan had to wear burqa. Political Islamic groups vigorously campaign to block reforms in women's civil rights in the Middle East and North Africa. As long as Islam secludes women from the public life, no real socio-economic progress is possible.

Prejudice in the Koran

The most despicable expression one can ever come across is that according to Hadith, women of heaven will be created in such a way that after each sexual intercourse, they will become virgin again. What a wild and naked misogyny! What an insult to women and to humans! Here, I quote Koranic verses about Huris, virgins and the sexist nature of Islam. These are few among many in the Koran:

52:17–20 "They will recline (with ease) on thrones arranged in ranks. And We shall marry them to Huris [beautiful maidens who await devout Muslim men in paradise] with wide lovely eye. There they shall pass from hand to hand a cup of wine."

37:40–48 "They will sit with bashful, dark-eyed virgins, as chaste as the sheltered eggs of ostriches."

44:52–55 "Yes and we shall wed them to dark-eyed beautiful virgins."

55:56–57 "In them will be bashful virgins neither man nor Jinn will have touched before. Then which of favourites of your Lord will you deny?"

78:31 "As for the righteous, they surely triumph. Their gardens and vineyards and high-breast virgins for companions, truly overflowing cup of wine."

78:33–34 "And young full-breasted (mature) maidens of equal age, and a full cup of wine." "Then which of the blessings of your Lord will you both (Jinn and men) deny? (In beauty) they are like rubies and corals."

56:7–40 "Owe created the Huris and made them virgins, loving companions for those on the right hands."

55:70–77 "In each there shall be virgins chaste and fair, dark-eyed virgins sheltered in their tents whom neither man nor Jinn have touched before."

56:22 "And there will be Huris with wide, lovely eyes as wives for the pious."

56:35–36 "Verily, We have created them (maidens) of special creation. And made them virgins."

40:45 "Surely for the God-fearing awaits a place of security gardens and vineyards and maidens with swelling breasts."

"The Huris are ever-young women who have wide eyes, flexing glances and swelling breasts."

Men have the absolute power of divorce

According to the Koran and Islamic law, a man has the right to terminate his marriage whenever and wherever he pleases. It is the absolute power of a Muslim male to repudiate his wife unilaterally at his discretion. He needs no reason for a divorce; a family quarrel or bad temper is sufficient. Divorce does not require any court, judge, lawyer, or counsellor. One phrase from a husband is enough to break the marriage bond: "you are divorced."

The Koran states: "If ye wish to exchange one wife for another." (4:20), giving the absolute power to the man to repudiate his wife and marry another without any formalities. In fact more than two dozens verses in Allah's scripture explain the modes of divorce (Koran 2: 226, 227, 228, 230–37, 241, 242; 4: 19–21, 130; 33: 49; 58: 3, 4; 63: 1–7; 4: 35). According to Islamic law, when a man wishes to divorce his wife, all he has to do is to say: "you are divorced," or "you are dismissed." In the second half of the 20th century, based on some legal changes in some of the Middle Eastern countries, men are required to be present in family courts and repudiate their wives before a judge. A man may divorce a wife and call her back up to three times. After the third repudiation, he cannot take her back again unless she marries and is separated from someone else first.

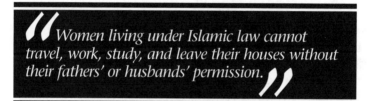

Women living under Islamic law cannot travel, work, study, and leave their houses without their fathers' or husbands' permission.

Fear of poverty keeps many women locked in bad marriages, as does the prospect of losing their children. Typically, fathers win custody of boys over the age of six and girls after the onset of puberty.

A woman can sue for divorce in the Islamic court on the specific grounds, such as the impotency of her husband, non-payment of maintenance, or his insanity. Cruelty is not sufficient grounds for divorce because wife beating is enjoined in the Koran. When a woman applies to the court for an injunction of divorce, and the husband is not willing to repudiate her, the procedure can be very lengthy and in most cases is futile.

The offering of financial consideration of some sort is commonly the repayment of the bride-price. When the marriage is contracted, a sum of money is stipulated to be paid by the husband to the wife or her male kinsmen before or after the wedding. This is called mahr (bride-price), which means marriage settlement or dowry. A man who divorces his wife must pay the full amount of the bride-price. When the wife agrees to buy her freedom, it is called khula in Arabic, which means something belonging to the wife is taken away from her. "There is no sin for either of them if the woman ransom herself." (Koran 2:229) The text of the scripture makes clear that the wife is actually paying money to her husband to get her freedom. This is ransom money, reminiscent of the ancient Arabian nomad's rite, which allowed the release of the booty or captive of the raids after receiving a ransom or head-price. Thus, in Islam a man actually buys his wife when he bargains over the bride-price (mahr) and sells his wife's freedom back to her when a financial settlement is paid for by her for a divorce. . . .

Women's lack of civil rights

Women living under Islamic law cannot travel, work, study, and leave their houses without their fathers' or husbands' permission. They do not have the right to choose the place of their residence. Under the terms of Koranic law, any judge fulfilling the seven requirements (that he have reached puberty, be a believer, know the Koranic laws perfectly, be just, and not be affected by amnesia, or not born illegitimate, or be of the female sex), is qualified to dispense justice in any type of cases. According to Islamic law, woman cannot choose her mate and is not permitted to divorce him. Her husband can divorce without her knowledge, and according to Shari'a, he is required to support her for only 100 days.

Polygamy and honour killing

According to the Koran a man can have four permanent wives and as many temporary wives as he wants:

2:3 "And of ye are apprehensive that ye shall not deal fairly with orphans, then, of other women who seem good in your eyes marry but two, or three or four, and if ye still fear that ye shall not act equitably, then one only; or the slaves whom ye have acquired."

Al-Nisa 4:24 "And all married women (are forbidden unto you) save those (captives) whom your right hand possess."

"Also (prohibited are) women already married except those whom your right hands possess."

33:52 "It is not lawful for thee (to marry more) women after this, nor to change them for (other) wives, even though their beauty attract thee, except any thy right hand should possess (as handmaidens): and Allah doth watch over all things."

Al-Nisa 4:34 "Marry such women as seem good to you, two, three, four; but if you fear you will not be equitable, then only one, or what your right hands own; so it is likelier you will not be partial."

23: 1,5,6 "Happy now the believers, humble is their prayers, shunning vain conversation, paying the poor-due, and who restrain their appetites except with their wives or the slaves whom their right hands possess: for in that case they shall be free from blame."

33:49–51 "O prophet! We allow thee thy wives whom thou hast dowered, and the slaves whom thy right hand possesseth out of the booty which God hath granted thee, and the daughters of thy uncles, thy paternal and maternal aunts who fled with thee to Medina, and any believing woman who hath given herself up to the Prophet, if the prophet desired to wed her—a privilege for thee above the rest of the Faithful. We well know what we have settled for them, in regard to their wives and to the slaves; that there may be no fault on thy part. Thou mayest decline for the present whom thou wilt of them, and thou mayest take to thy bed her whom thou wilt, and whomsoever thou shalt long for those thou shalt have before neglected, and this shall not be a crime in thee."

Honour killings are an example of a practice that is commonly associated with Islam. It has broader root and has been incorporated into Islamic rules and Islamic law; Shari'a. It is based in tribal culture, in which a family's authority and ultimately its survival is tightly linked to its honour. Muslim perpetrators repeatedly justify their crime by referring to the Koran that states harsh punishments for adultery.

The just fight against Islam

Civilised humanity has slowly moved towards the equal treatment of women and the recognition of women's equal rights. Religions are one of the oldest and the most persistent obstacles on the way of women's equality and freedom. Indeed, religion is women's enemy and it is the nature of all religions particularly Islam to look backwards to past ancient times and antiquated values. Women will be universally equal someday, when that day comes, it will arrive in spite of all religions and as a result of a just and powerful fight against Islam.

3

The Koran Teaches That Women Cannot Be Leaders

Moulana Muhammad Karolia

Moulana Muhammad Karolia teaches at Jameah Mahmoodiyah Springs, an Islamic school in South Africa. He has served as an imam (religious leader) and is the author of a number of booklets about various Islamic topics.

According to the Koran, women have different rights than men because of women's natural inferiority. Women are physically weak and deficient in intellect. In addition, women cannot perform the required prayers during their menstrual periods and are therefore both unclean and less pious than men are. Women are also dependent on men for financial support and dowries. Women cannot be leaders because of these inferior qualities.

Female leadership is a question not unknown to the Muslim world. Although Muslim scholars have in the past discussed this topic, it first gained prominence in the twentieth century with the wake of the women's liberty movement. In recent years the question was further highlighted with the success of Benazir Bhutto in the 1989 elections in Pakistan and Khalida Zia in the 1991 election in Bangladesh.[1] . . .

Prior to Islam, women were among the most oppressed

---

1. Benazir Bhutto was elected prime minister of Pakistan in 1989. Khalida Zia was elected president of Bangladesh in 1991.

creatures in the world. Neither did they have any rights nor were they regarded as human-beings in many communities.

Woman's rights

Islam on the contrary, raised the social status of a woman and granted her many rights ranging from inheritance to the basic necessities of everyday-life. Regarding these rights Allâh Ta'âla[2] says in the Qurân: "And women have rights similar to the rights against them (i.e. the right of men) according to what is equitable and men have a degree over them."

Mufti Muhammad Shafi Saheb (RA)[3] explains this verse: "The rights of women that men are responsible for are compulsory just as the rights of men that women are responsible for are compulsory. The right of both (men and women) have been given the same ruling . . . it is not necessary that the rights of both take the same form. Instead, if women are responsible for a specific duty then so are men. Household matters, training and looking after the children are the responsibility of the women whereas men are responsible for earning a living so that they may fulfil the needs of women (their wives). It is a lady's duty to serve and obey her husband and the *mehr* (dowry) and expenditure of the women is the husband's duty. . . . There is however one quality on accord of which men have superiority over women. This is why Allâh Ta'âla, at the end of this verse says: *"and men have a degree over them."*

> *Women are deficient in intellect and deen.*

Mufti Shafi (RA) thereafter explains that this degree of superiority that men have over women is explained in the verse: "Men are overseers of women because Allâh Ta'âla granted virtue to some of them (i.e. men) over others (i.e. women) and because of their spending from their wealth".

Shaikh Muhammad Rashid Rida offers a similar explana-

2. Allâh Ta'âla means "Allah is pure and exalted." This is an expression that Muslims use whenever the name of Allah is pronounced or written.   3. RA is an abbreviation for Radhiallahu 'anhu, meaning "May Allah be pleased with him." This expression is a sign of respect to be used by Muslims whenever a name of a companion of the Prophet Muhammad is mentioned or used in writing.

tion: ". . . the lady equals the man in all rights (i.e. in the ruling of all rights) except one which Allâh refers to in the sentence 'and men have a degree over them.' This degree is explained in the verse "men are overseers.'. . ."

Women had been created as the weaker sex.

It is therefore necessary that we now focus our attention on this verse of the Qurân in the list of some acclaimed commentators of the Qurân.

Men are overseers of women

Llamah Ibn-ul-Arabi (RA) comments on this verse:

The meaning of this verse is: I have made men overseers of women because I have granted the former superiority over the latter. This is due to three reasons:

a. perfect understanding

b. perfection of deen[4] and obedience in jihad and commanding the good and forbidding the evil etc. This has been explained by Nabi sallallahu alaihi wasallam[5] in an authentic Hadith [scripture]:

"I have not seen any one of deficient intellect and deen who is more destructive to the intelligence of a cautious man than you women."

The women asked: "Why is that, O messenger of Allâh?" He replied: "Do you not spend a few nights without performing salâh [prayer] and without keeping fast?" This is the deficiency of her deen and the testimony of one of you equals half the testimony of a single man—this is the deficiency of her intellect. ". . . so that if one of the two women errs, the second would remind her".

c. His spending on her in the form of dowry and other expenditure.

Allamah Âlusi (RA) writes in the commentary of this verse that it is the quality of men to oversee the affairs of women just

---

4. Deen is piety.   5. Sallallahu alaihi wasallam means "May the blessings and the peace of Allah be upon him."

as the rulers oversee their subjects by commanding them to do good. . . .

a. because Allâh has granted him superiority as has been narrated (in the Hadith) that women are deficient in intellect and deen and men are the opposite . . .

b. because men bear the expenditure of women. . . .

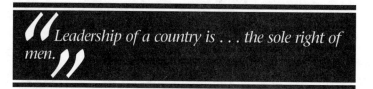

Leadership of a country is . . . the sole right of men.

Commenting on the verse "men are overseers. . . ." Maulana Shabeer Saheb Uthmani (RA) writes: "It was mentioned in the previous verse that the rights of men and women have been given full consideration. Had their rights been given a different consideration (women's rights were not considered [as] fully as men's rights) women would be justified in complaining. This verse now explains that men have a status higher than women, women cannot complain because the difference of rules (regarding men and women) that result on accord of this additional degree of men is in total agreement with divine wisdom."

Men and women do not have the same rights

Just a few commentaries of the verses concerned have been mentioned above. Many other commentators have elucidated the meaning of these verses in a similar manner. The above discussions may be summarised in the following points:

- Although both men and women have rights upon each other that are compulsory, their rights do differ in many situations.
- Men have an additional right over women—they are their overseers and guardians.
- There are two reasons due to which men have been given this additional right over women. Firstly, they have to give the women their dowries and they are responsible for all their expenses. Secondly, Allâh granted man this favour when creating him, women had been created as the weaker sex. Besides, women experience monthly menstrual periods due to which they are unable to perform salâh and fast during that period. Thus the Hadith

has classified her as deficient in deen. The Hadith has in a similar vein regarded her as deficient in intellect because the Qurân has regarded the testimony of one lady equal to half the testimony of a single man.

- Since the rights of women have been given the same amount of importance and consideration as the rights of men, women should not complain of men having an additional right over them. If they do, they would be questioning the wisdom of Allâh.

It may thus be concluded that although men and women are equal in that both have rights, they do not have the same rights. Among the sole rights of a male is that he is always the head of a family since he is the guardian of the women. Leadership of a country is . . . the sole right of men.

4

Islamic Tradition Proves That Women Have the Right to Be Leaders

Moodhy Al-Khalaf

Moodhy Al-Khalaf is a Saudi journalist based in Riyadh.

Muslims who argue that women are not allowed to be leaders often cite one hadith, or scripture, as evidence. However, critical analyses of this hadith reveal that it may not be authentic or that it has been misinterpreted. Muslim women throughout history have served as leaders who were accepted and respected by the scholars in their community. Modern Islamic women are asking for the right to become whatever their abilities enable them to be.

In a heated debate with a male relative about one of my articles, he snaps: "Next you'll be asking to be a minister!" I stop for a second: "Why not?" What is so shocking about a woman minister, political consultant, a member of the Shoura Council,[1] ambassador or judge? I still cannot understand why men in my country insist on viewing women as inferior. I still cannot believe that they do not see that women have proven their capabilities in many fields. Political leadership is no exception.

When Muslim men are asked why they object to women in politics, they usually quote one particular Hadith: "A nation which places its affairs in the hands of a woman shall never prosper!" Let us examine this Hadith first in its context. If the

1. council that advises the king of Saudi Arabia

Prophet [Muhammad] (peace be upon him) actually did say this, it was upon hearing that the Persians had appointed Chosroe's[2] daughter as ruler. He was probably predicting the fall of the dynasty—not disenfranchising women.

Scholars will agree that there are several Hadiths of this type; i.e. limited to certain events which do not include any kind of later application. If he was undermining the role of women as leaders, would he contradict himself by telling his followers that a third of their religion could be learned from Aisha (his wife)?

I say "if the Prophet actually said this," because several scholars have found reasons to reject its authenticity. First of all, the narrator of the Hadith is Abu Bakrah, a man who was convicted of, and flogged for, false testimony during [seventh-century ruler] Caliph Omar's reign. Hence, according to Islamic law, his narration of Hadith should not be accepted. Moreover, the context in which he first mentions the Hadith is even more perplexing: Abu Bakrah had sided with [Muhammad's wife] Aisha and her troops against Ali [the Prophet's nephew] in the "Battle of the Camel." After her defeat and return to Madinah he narrated the Hadith.

Islamic history is rich in women leaders.

Scholars who reject this Hadith say that this companion could not have understood the Prophet's words as an injunction against female leadership. If that were the case, then he would be in an awkward position. It is not possible that a true companion would remember an injunction of the Prophet and proceed to disobey it. Nor would he be so disrespectful as to announce subsequently the recollection without explaining why he ignored it.

Actions of the Prophet

Leaving that Hadith aside, let us examine the Prophet's political history with women. Actions speak louder than words, and Islamic history is rich in women leaders. Two women were

2. king of Persia from A.D. 590 to 628

among the first people to come and secretly pledge their allegiance to the Prophet. Later, after the Prophet returned to Makkah, he was approached by dozens of men pledging allegiance, and many women came as well. He did not turn them away or ask them to send their male guardians to pledge allegiance on their behalf.

The Qur'an says: "O Prophet! Whenever believing women come unto thee to pledge their allegiance to thee . . . then accept their pledge of allegiance." (60:12) This is the equivalent to voting today. Over 1,400 years ago, Muslim women were already allowed to vote. They continued to do so during the reigns of subsequent rulers. What has become of us today? Not one Saudi woman is a member of the Shoura or has a say in any political matter.

Islam is not a chauvinistic religion; it never was and never should be.

What about women who were even more politically active in Islamic history? The first martyr in Islam, Sumaya, was a woman. Moreover, women fought in battles, side by side even with the Prophet. Two prominent examples of this are Umm Imara and Nasiba bint Kaab. Omar, the second caliph, narrates: "I heard the Prophet saying: 'On the day of Uhud, I never looked right or left without seeing Umm Imara fighting to defend me.'" As for Nasiba bint Kaab, she fought alongside both the Prophet and the first caliph, Abu Bakr. She was such a distinguished and courageous warrior that the caliph himself attended her reception on her return to Madinah.

If women in Islam were meant to lead the kind of marginalized lives we lead today, why didn't anyone tell these women to stay home? Are we claiming to know better than the Prophet and his companions?

The Prophet's wives played strong political roles

The Prophet's wives were also politically active. Umm Salamah was instrumental in advising the Prophet during the crisis of Hudaibiyah. Her advice prevented disunity and prevailed over the advice of other men including Omar ibn Al-Khattab. Aisha was a rich source of religious knowledge and the first Muslim woman to lead men into battle. She is the epitome of a woman leader. If women were not meant to be leaders, why are some of the Prophet's wives so politically inspiring?

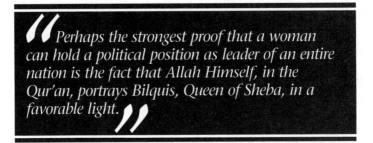

Perhaps the strongest proof that a woman can hold a political position as leader of an entire nation is the fact that Allah Himself, in the Qur'an, portrays Bilquis, Queen of Sheba, in a favorable light.

The earliest woman actually to hold a governmental position was probably Al-Shafa bint Abdullah ibn Abd Shams whom the second caliph appointed manager of the market at Madinah. She supervised men and women and had authority over both. Could the Prophet's close companion be wrong in giving such an example? Are we better and more pious than Omar? If not, then why don't we have a single politically appointed position where a woman has authority over a man? Even in our purely female academic institutions, the chain always goes back to a man who has the last word. Islam is not a chauvinistic religion; it never was and never should be.

Islamic women were also religious leaders

And what about women as religious authorities? One of the most powerful positions in early and contemporary Islam is that of judge. Why does the mere mention of such a topic cause such problems? What do our early religious scholars think of women being judges? Ibn Hazm, a prominent traditional scholar, was of the opinion that women could be judges in all kinds of cases. He relied on the following Qur'anic verse "Behold, God bids you to deliver all that you have been entrusted with unto those who are entitled thereto, and whenever you judge between people, to judge with justice. Verily, most excellent is what God exhorts you to do: verily, God is all-hearing, all-seeing!" (4:58); Ibn Hazm said that since this verse addressed both men and women, there was no need to discriminate between the two.

Imam Abu Hanifah similarly believed that women could be

judges but only on issues regarding domestic/family law. Despite these examples, we do not have a single female judge in Saudi Arabia. Are these imams not the same religious authorities that we resort to in other religious matters? Why are we selective in what we use and what we refuse? And, if this is the case, who decides what to use and what to refuse?

The example of Allah himself

Perhaps the strongest proof that a woman can hold a political position as leader of an entire nation is the fact that Allah Himself, in the Qur'an, portrays Bilquis, Queen of Sheba, in a favorable light. We are told the story of a strong woman who is a democratic ruler, consulting her people before making important decisions. After witnessing Solomon's power, she becomes a believer and remains the Queen of Sheba. We as Muslims know that when we are told a story in the Qur'an, it is not for entertainment but for our education. If it was wrong for a woman to be a leader, would Allah fail to mention that crucial point?

In conclusion, I must admit that my relative was absolutely right: I am asking for the right to be a minister. I am asking for the right to be whatever my abilities may enable me to be.

5

Islamic Women in South Asia Must Fight for Economic Independence

Benazir Bhutto

Benazir Bhutto was the first woman ever to lead a modern Islamic nation. She served as prime minister of Pakistan from 1988 to 1990 and from 1993 to 1996. She is currently the head of the Pakistan People's Party.

The majority of women in South Asia face discrimination and exploitation. This injustice is not the fault of Islam but of patriarchal traditions that keep women subservient to men. To break these chains of subservience, women need to attain economic liberty, which includes access to education, the freedom to work, and the right to control property. While Bhutto's government made many strides in the cause of woman's rights in Pakistan in the 1990s, the current government is repressing women. The leaders of South Asia must act to empower women with just laws, economic opportunities, and strong role models.

Editor's note: This selection is an extract from a speech by Benazir Bhutto to the Council of Indian Industry on November 26, 2001, in New Delhi. The council is a business association that was founded more than a century ago.

Benazir Bhutto, address to the Council of Indian Industry, New Delhi, India, November 26, 2001.

B y your focus on the essential rights of woman in society, you support the voice of the powerless, the exploited, and the abused. For women, despite the strides taken in the last century, are still the most powerless and exploited group in the world community. For me, the cause of women, is God's most noble cause, the cause of justice, equality, and life. . . .

It is impossible to separate women's rights from human rights, just as it is impossible to separate economic justice from political liberty. In the modern era, these issues are the essential operationalizations of morality, of civility, of a just society.

I come before you with a unique double focus. On one level, as the victim of human rights violations today and in the past, and on another level as someone who has had the extraordinary opportunity to address women's rights in my own country [Pakistan]. I am no stranger to the issues of women's empowerment. I wear the scars, on my body and my soul, of the abuse of basic human rights, and thus I view oppression through the eyes of the victim.

We do not live in a perfect world, and even amongst the rapidly expanding democratic community there often seems coldness, indifference, hypocrisy and lingering prejudice. Many thought heaven would appear on earth with the crumbling of the Berlin Wall. A decade later we find that Europe may be united, but the cause of justice of the discriminated people in many countries is far from complete.

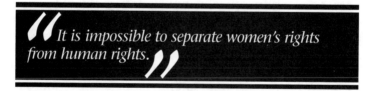

It is impossible to separate women's rights from human rights.

Let us be truthful, the world will be a fair place when each and every human being on our planet is treated equally. And there is no human right more fundamental, and more universal, than equal rights for woman in the new century. Democracy is the first step toward humanity's liberation. But it is not an end in itself.

Liberty depends on social and economic justice, and above all on the universal, non-selective application of human rights to all citizens of the world. Economic development and political development are surely linked, but both are predicated on guaranteed human rights.

Women's place in Islam

As the first woman ever elected to head an Islamic nation, I feel a special responsibility about issues that relate to women. I am often asked about the place of women in the message of Islam. For me, the discrimination against women has little to do with Islam and more to do with custom and tradition. Here in South Asia, many of the women in the ethnically and religiously diverse countries suffer similar fates. Too many are denied the right to live fully. Too often, women are seen as extensions of the male rather than as individuals in their own right.

One of the difficulties I encounter is the prejudice born of centuries that a woman is the property of the man. Here I am an independent woman, educated in modern universities, the daughter of an emancipated leader and I find myself the center of controversy in the minds of the traditionalists. For them, my husband is to blame for letting me work. Traditionally respected men did not allow their wives to work. By that definition, in their eyes, my husband must be something other than a respectable person. They punish him, to punish me, and in seeking to punish us, they seek to punish women, and men who see women as separate legal entities, everywhere.

The battle with the traditionalists is a battle that has dogged my political career. During the general elections in 1988, the opposition claimed that those voters who cast their vote for me would have their marriage vows dissolved in the eyes of God. Such hysterical denunciation of a woman seeking the highest electoral office highlights some of the prejudices that women in South Asia face as they seek political and economic empowerment.

South Asia is home to some of the deepest prejudices that exist against women. Honour killings[1] and gas stove murders of women are the extreme manifestations of the prejudices against women. Yet South Asia is home to the largest number of women elected in any place and at any time in the world community. Sri Lanka's Mrs. [Chandrika] Bandernaike led the way with her election as Prime Minister. This was followed by the election of India's Mrs. Indira Gandhi. Pakistan and Bangladesh came next.

---

1. Honour killings occur when a male family member kills a woman relative because she is suspected of improper relations with a man to whom she is not married. Improper actions can be as minor as having telephone conversations, exchanging glances that are considered to be flirtatious, and being seen walking next to a man.

Bangladesh went one step forward in having a leader of the house and leader of the Opposition from the same gender.

The rise of women leaders in South Asia often reinforces the traditionalist view that women are extensions of their menfolk. We are often told that we got where we did because of who we were related to, rather than inherent qualities. The leading men in our father's lives called Mrs. Gandhi "Guryha" (doll) and I was called "that girl". Yet it would be half the story to write of us as extensions of the male members of the family. There were other men in our families, some of whom did come forward to contest and compete. It's important to recognise that each woman leader in South Asia had something within her which enabled her to succeed. Family name is important and character is important too. In South Asia, the rights of women have more to do with the social class they belong to. Women from privileged classes live life according to different standards than those of other classes. For me, the empowerment of women lies less in laws and more in economic independence. And it lies also in men. Our fathers who encourage us. Our male colleagues who stand by us. Our male followers who support us and the male citizens who vote for us. Dependent women, like dependent nations, are not free to take the decisions they may like to take. For them survival becomes the code with which to address their situation.

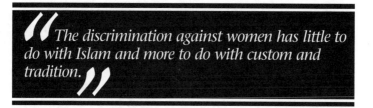

The discrimination against women has little to do with Islam and more to do with custom and tradition.

I was reminded about this starkly when Pakistan's military regime justified joining the international coalition against terror on grounds of survival. The military regime said it feared that its nuclear assets and other strategic concerns could be endangered if it failed to join up. That is not the way I would have put it. Yet it illustrates two points. First that, women often make pragmatic choices because they are yet to become free. Second, that even men put survival before other issues which shows that the strength of the social background matters where freedom is concerned. We are all born free, as [French writer Jean-Jacques] Rousseau said, yet too many of us are in chains.

These chains come from the state or they come from the mind. These chains can be broken if we will it. It's important for South Asia to break the chains that hold its women back. . . .

The importance of women's leadership

This is a time when women's leadership, at all levels of society, is all the more important. . . . For women to succeed, job opportunities and avenues are needed. Respect for the fundamental rights for women will flow when woman have the economic means to stand up for themselves.

The government I led did its best for women. We recruited Lady Health Workers, an army of them, to reduce population growth rate and infant mortality rate. We hired new teachers for our primary schools and seventy per cent of them were women. We set up a women's bank run only by women for women although men were allowed to put their money in the accounts. We ran advertisements asking women to report husbands who beat them to the police stations. We appointed women judges to the superior judiciary for the first time in our history. We established women's police stations which women could visit with confidence. We lifted the ban on women taking part in sports. We hosted a Women's Olympics and held the first meeting of the Parliamentarian for Muslim women.

And because I was a woman, every woman felt protected. Not a single case of honour killings was reported during my tenure after we arrested a man who burnt his wife with electric wires in 1994. . . .

The repression of women has returned

Today in Pakistan, the veil of repression has descended across our people. The cause of human rights is being set back decades. But the cause of women's rights, I am sad to say, is being set back a century. . . .

It saddens me to see the price the women of Pakistan paid for the dismissal of the democratic government[2] I led. It is particularly heartbreaking to see the dismantlement of the array of special programs that I instituted in my two terms as Prime

2. Bhutto fell from power in 1996 amid charges of corruption and murder. She contended that the charges were politically motivated and has continued to lead the Pakistan People's Party from exile in England.

Minister to raise the quality of life of women in Pakistan.

My departure led to the collapse of national revenues, investment and growth. And the money for people welfare programs was simply not there. Of those programs, the programs for women, the weakest of the social classes, were hit first.

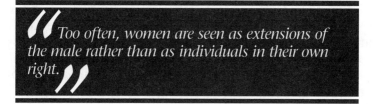

Too often, women are seen as extensions of the male rather than as individuals in their own right.

The women of South Asia cannot be expected to struggle alone against the forces of discrimination, exploitation and manipulation. I recall the words of [Italian writer] Dante who reminded us that "The hottest place in Hell is reserved for those who remain neutral in times of moral crisis." Today in this world, in the fight for the liberation of women, there can be no neutrality. Our outrage at violence and discrimination directed at women cannot be selective. Hate, bigotry and violence have no international borders. Every shamed, abused girl, wherever she lives, is a mute witness for all women, everywhere in the world.

A vision of woman's rights

I speak at a time when new forces shape the new century, the new millennium. We shape a world committed to universal social, economic and political values—this triangular definition of comprehensive human rights for the future. We must shape a world free from exploitation and maltreatment of women. A world in which women have opportunities to rise to the highest level in business, diplomacy, and other spheres of life. Where there are no battered women. Where honour and dignity are protected in peace, and in war. Where women have economic freedom and independence. Where women are equal partners in peace and development.

Repressive forces always will stand ready to exploit the moment and push us back into the past. Let us remember the words of the German writer, Goethe: "Freedom has been remade and re-earned in every generation."

The women of South Asia will not be free, until we determine to empower them. Empower them with words, with laws, with awareness, with economic opportunities and with role models. . . . We are not free if girls cannot read. For a girl who cannot read has no future; and a girl with no future has no human rights.

In this elegant city, we must remember that in the time it took for me to address you today, over one thousand children have starved to death on this planet. As long as these basic violations of human rights are allowed to continue, none of us—regardless of where we live, regardless of how civilized our lifestyles, regardless of our own personal circumstances and comforts—none of us are free. . . .

My inspiration

My commitment to the rights of women was inspired by the categorical position taken by Pakistan's founder, Quaid-e-Azam Mohammad Ali Jinnah.

In his address to the university students in 1944, he said, "No nation can rise to the heights of glory with half its population shackled. It is a crime against humanity that our women are confined within the four walls of their homes like prisoners; they should be side by side with men as their companions in all spheres of life."

I will end with a quote from [English poet] Alexander Pope who said:

> "What war could ravish,
> Commerce could bestow
> And he returned a friend
> Who was a foe."

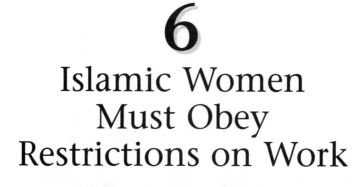

6

Islamic Women Must Obey Restrictions on Work

Yusuf Al Qaradawy

Yusuf Al Qaradawy is the dean of the faculty of Islamic ju-
risprudence and Islamic studies at the University of Qatar.
He has written extensively on Islamic law and social issues.
He is a commentator for the Al-Jazeera television network,
the Arabic language channel that originates in Qatar.

A woman's primary sphere of activity is the home. All
other activities are secondary to her role as wife and
mother. Women are permitted to work outside the
home only if their work does not interfere with their
domestic duties. They are limited in the types of work
that is permitted to them. Women may only take positions where they do not have to interact with men,
such as teaching in all-girls schools or giving medical
treatments to women.

I slam considers the home as the great kingdom of the woman.
She is its mistress, its head and axis. She is the man's wife, his
partner, the solace of his loneliness, and the mother of his children. Islam considers a woman's job of keeping house, looking
after her husband's affairs, and raising her children well as a
kind of worship ('ibaadah) and struggle in the cause of Allah (jihad). Therefore, it resists every method or system that hampers
her from fulfilling her task or that impairs her from performing
her duty in the best way or that destroys her home.

Every method or system that attempts to remove the woman

from her kingdom, to take her from her husband, or displace her from her children in the name of freedom, work, art, etc., is in fact the woman's foe that wants to rob her of everything and hardly give her anything. Doubtless, it is rejected by Islam.

Islam wants to establish happy homes to be the basis of a happy society. Happy homes are established on confidence and certainty, not on doubts and suspicion. The family whose consistency is based on a couple exchanging suspicions and fears is a family on the edge of an abyss, a family for which life is an unbearable hell.

Islam considers the home as the great kingdom of the woman.

Islam allows her to work outside the home in an appropriate job which suits her nature, her concern, and her capacity, and which does not crush her femininity. Her work is legitimate within certain limits and certain conditions, especially when she or her family needs the outside work or when the society itself needs her work in particular. The need for work is not merely limited to the financial aspect. It could be a psychological need such as the need of a specialised learned woman who is not married, or the married woman who has no children, or who has a lot of leisure time and to alleviate boredom.

The matter is not as claimed by those who are for the woman's work without any limitations or controls. We will deal with this topic in some details in the next pages, Allah willing. . . .

Ill-conceived justifications for women to work

The cunning and slyness is frequently shown in not declaring outright what is wanted is woman to rebel against her nature, exceed the limits of her femininity and make use of that femininity for illicit pleasure or illicit earning. They appear in the image of pure and loyal people who do not seek anything but the general interest. Opinions concerning the work of the woman are stressed through scattered reasons, collected as follows

1. The West, which is more advanced than us in civilisation, has preceded us in employing women; so, if we wish to advance like the West, we should follow suit in everything, for

civilisation is an integrated whole.

2. Women represent half the society. If they stay at home without employment, it is a waste, and it has harmful effects on the national economy. It is in the interest of the society for women to work.

3. It is also in the interest of the family for the woman to work, as the costs of living have increased in our age. The woman's employment increases the family's income and helps the man with expenses of living, especially in an environment where income is limited.

4. It is in the interest of the woman herself for her to work. Coming into contact with people and life, with the society outside the home, polishes her personality and provides her with experiences she would never have obtained inside her home.

5. In addition, work is a weapon to arm her against the enmity of time. Her father might pass away, her husband might divorce her, or she might be neglected by her children. In that case, she would not be humiliated by poverty and need, especially at a time characterised by selfishness, widespread ingratitude, and cut-off blood relations in which everyone is merely concerned about himself. . . .

Misconceptions in the Western view of women

As to the claim of the West, it is a false claim for the following reasons:

1. The West is not a good example for us to follow, and we are not committed to take the West as . . . worshippers of Allah or as a model to be followed. "To you your religion and to me my religion (Islamic Monotheism)". [Surah 109:6]

2. In the West the woman has been forced to go to the factory, the store, etc. and does not do so out of her own choice. She is driven by the need of food and is obliged to earn her living after being rejected by man, who refuses to be in charge in a cruel and merciless society which does not have mercy for the young nor for the weak females. Allah has provided us with the maintenance system in our Islamic Law, which makes such action unnecessary for the woman. . . .

3. The West which is followed as a model has been complaining now of woman's work and its consequences. Women themselves are complaining of such misfortune on which they have no choice. . . .

4. It is not in the interest of the society [for a woman] to

abandon her first calling at home to work as engineer, or a lawyer, or a representative, or a judge, or a factory worker; but it is in its interest for her work in the field of her specialisation for which she is instinctually prepared, the field of marital life and motherhood, which is not less serious but more so than working in stores, laboratories and establishments. Napoleon was asked, "Which castles of France are more impregnable?" He said, "Good mothers."

Many have undermined the work of the house wife which is one of the greatest services to the community. The responsibilities of a home and children are abundant and challenging. The woman has the task of homemaking, which entails a lot of physical labour, and the job of shaping her children to be productive citizens. If some women have some leisure time, it can be spent doing crafts, serving their communities and their fellow women, or contributing to fighting poverty, ignorance and vice.

In fact, a lot of working women employ other women as baby-sitters for their children or as servants at home. This means that the house needs a woman to look after its affairs, and the priority goes to its mistress and queen instead of to the outsider, who in most cases [is] a stranger to the house with different morals, religion, language, ideas and habits, as is prevalent in the Gulf societies where nannies and servants are imported from the Far East. The danger of that situation cannot be hidden from the sane person.

5. The happiness of the family rests not in merely increasing the income—which is mostly spent on buying clothes for going to work, and necessities for a mixed life (e.g. men mixing with women) which is based on affectation, the fashion race and being in vogue. In return, the home is deprived of the quietude and companionship established by the woman in the atmosphere of the family. The working woman is exhausted, quick-tempered, and needs someone to lessen her burden, so she cannot give what she has not got to the home.

6. It is not in the interest of the woman to force her out of her nature and her responsibility and force her to do a man's work. Allah has created her a female. To do a man's work, then, is cheating her nature and reality. A woman could gradually lose her femininity until she is what some English writers have called the "third sex". That is what many women of moral courage have confessed.

7. What is claimed as weapon in the hand of the woman, if it works in the West, does not work for us as Muslims. This is

because in Islam a woman has her needs satisfied due to the obligatory maintenance decreed by Islamic Law on her father, or her husband, or sons, or brothers, or others of blood relation. If copying the West has started to make us gradually lose our traits so that even the brother has started to deny his sister, the male relative has started to abandon his duty towards his female relative, and many people think merely of themselves, we still must adhere to Allah's Laws until the religious motive supersedes the worldly motives. . . .

The harmful effects of women doing men's work

Therefore we learn that when the woman is involved in men's work without restrictions or limits, it has its harmful effect on various aspects:

1. It is harmful for the woman herself because she loses her femininity and her distinguishing characteristics and is deprived of her home and children. Some become barren and some are like "the third sex", which is neither a man nor a woman.

2. It is harmful for the husband because he is deprived of a bounteous source flowing with good company and cheerfulness. Nothing flows any longer except arguments and complaints about the troubles of work, the rivalry of work mates, men and women. This is in addition to the jealousy the man may feel, real or imagined, of other men in the workplace who vie for her attention.

3. It has a harmful effect on children because a mother's compassion, sympathy and supervision cannot be compensated by a servant or a teacher. How can children get benefit from a mother spending her day at work and on her arrival at home being tired and stressed? Neither her physical nor her psychological condition would allow the best she has to give regarding education or direction to her children.

4. It is harmful for men because every working woman takes the position of an eligible working man. As long as there are unemployed men in the society, the woman's work is harmful to them.

5. It is harmful for the work itself because women are frequently absent from their work due to natural emergencies which cannot be avoided, as menstruation, giving birth, nursing a baby, and the like. All such things deprive the work of discipline and valuable output.

6. It is harmful on morals. It is harmful to the woman's morals if she loses her modesty and on the man if he loses his attentiveness. It is harmful on the whole society if earning a living and increasing the income is the main goal sought by people, disregarding higher principles and good models.

7. It is harmful on social life because going against the grains of nature and dislocating things which are naturally located spoils life itself and causes imbalance, disorder and chaos. . . .

Permissible work for women

Do we understand that the woman's work is forbidden by Allah in any case? Certainly not. However, here we have to indicate to what extent and in which fields the Islamic Law allows the woman to work. That is what we are going to point out briefly and clearly, so that the right will not be mixed with the wrong on this sensitive issue.

The woman's first and greatest work, in which no one can rival her, is to rear new generations . . .

That does not signify that the woman's work outside her home is forbidden by Islamic Law. No one has the right to forbid without an authentic text which is clear in meaning. On that basis, we say that the woman's work in itself is allowed. It is even requested if she is in need of it, if she is a widow, divorced, or did not have a chance to marry, and if she has no income to avoid the humility of asking for charity or people's condescension. It could be the family who needs her work, such as to help her husband, or to care for her children, or young brothers and sisters, or her father in his old age. . . .

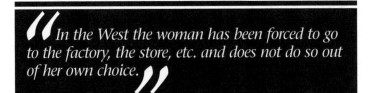

In the West the woman has been forced to go to the factory, the store, etc. and does not do so out of her own choice.

The society itself might be in need of the woman's work, as in giving medical treatment to women and looking after them, teaching girls and such work that concerns women. It is more proper for a woman to deal with another woman like herself, instead of with a man. The acceptance of a man in some cases is a matter of necessity which should be considered accordingly and should not be taken as a rule. The same case applies when the society needs working hands for the sake of development. If we allow some women to work, it should be restricted by a number of conditions:

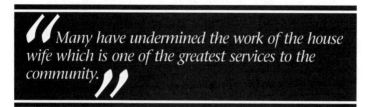

Many have undermined the work of the house wife which is one of the greatest services to the community.

1. The work itself should be Islamically lawful in the sense that it should not be Islamically forbidden (haram) or lead to what is forbidden, for instance as a maid working in the house of a bachelor, or as a private secretary for a manager, whose position requires her to stay with him alone, or as a dancer who excites physical instincts and lusts, or as a worker in a restaurant serving alcohol. The Prophet (blessings and peace be upon him) condemned those who produce alcohol as well as those who transport or sell it. She should not work as an air hostess, a position which obliges her to wear forbidden clothes and offer what is unlawful (haram) to passengers. Her job would also require her to stay overnight alone in foreign countries, some of which are not safe. She should not work in other types of work forbidden by Islam for women in particular, or forbidden for men or women.

2. If she goes out of her house, she should adhere to the morals of a Muslim woman in her clothing, her talk and movement. "And tell the believing women to lower their gaze (from looking at forbidden things), and protect their private parts (from illegal sexual acts) and not to show off their adornment except only that which is apparent and let them not stamp their feet so as to reveal what they hide of their adornment. . . .

3. Her work should not affect other duties which cannot be neglected, such as her duty towards her children and husband, which is her foremost and basic duty. . . .

4. What is required of the Muslim community is to organise matters and make arrangements so that the Muslim woman can work—if her interest or her family's or her society's requires that—without touching her modesty, or contradicting her commitment towards Allah, herself or her home. The general atmosphere should help her to perform her tasks as well as ob-

tain her rights. There should be some arrangements where she can work part-time for half pay (three days a week, for example). She should also be granted enough leave for her marriage, delivery and nursing.

5. Some of the arrangements should include setting schools, colleges and universities especially for girls where they can practise sports and physical exercises suitable for them and where they can have freedom of movement to practise different activities. There should also be women in ministries, establishments and banks, away from places of temptation and where a woman will not be alone with one or more men, in addition to other and new means which cannot be counted.

It is Allah Who says the truth and guides to the right path.

7

The Traditional Islamic View of Sexuality Benefits Women

Madeleine Bunting

Madeleine Bunting is a senior correspondent with the Guardian *newspaper in the United Kingdom.*

Educated Islamic women who live in the United Kingdom discuss their opinions about the position of women in Islam, all agreeing that their religion has liberated and empowered them. They share their personal experiences in donning the *hijab*, or Islamic veil, stating that they do not consider it a form of repression. They do not wish to express their sexuality in public, and the veil allows them to guard their modesty. For them, the battle of Western feminists to assert the power of female sexuality is pointless because they feel Islamic women already have a healthy acceptance of sexuality. They also prefer a degree of segregation from men because it allows them to avoid the confusing ambiguities of friendships with men.

We're sitting in a stylish club, ArRum, in Clerkenwell, central London. Firelight is flickering on the leather sofas, there is contemporary art on the walls and delicious "fusion" food on the table, but what distinguishes this club from its many neighbours is that it is Muslim, there is no alcohol on the menu and downstairs there's a prayer room. The stylish place conveys a complex ethos—modern, yet true to its Muslim identity.

A suitable setting, then, chosen by the six Muslim women

who agreed to meet me to discuss Islam and the position of women. All university graduates, all in their mid-twenties in careers ranging from journalism to teaching, all have chosen in the past few years to wear the hijab (a scarf wrapped tightly around their heads to conceal every wisp of hair). Most strikingly, however, all of these women fluently and cogently articulate how they believe Islam has liberated and empowered them. The Islam they describe is a million miles away from that of the Taliban,[1] let alone the Islam practised in many Muslim countries from Pakistan to Saudi Arabia, but they insist—and back up their points with Koranic references—that the Islam they first discovered when they were teenagers is true to the Prophet's teachings. They don't need western feminism, which, they argue, developed as a reaction against the particular expression of western patriarchy.

Within the Koranic tradition and the life of the Prophet lie the rights and inspiration a woman needs to achieve her full potential—the challenge ahead is to educate Muslim girls and women so that they have that knowledge. They justify wearing the hijab, either as a public statement of their own spiritual quest, or of their political identity in a world where Islam perceives itself as under threat, or both.

> // *Within the Koranic tradition and the life of the Prophet lie the rights and inspiration a woman needs to achieve her full potential.* //

Shagufta, the 25-year-old editor of the Muslim magazine *Q News*, was brought up in London, in a traditional Pakistani home where the emphasis was on cultural conservatism rather than piety. A marriage to a cousin from Pakistan was arranged for her when she was about 10. Her parents had no wish for her to continue her education, and her adoption of the hijab was her rebellion against this traditional cultural background. "When I first put on hijab, my parents were shocked," she says.

1. The Taliban ruled Afghanistan from 1996 to 2001. It instituted a brutal conservative Islamic regime under which women were not allowed to leave their homes without a male relative accompanying them; were denied employment, medical care, and education; and were forced to wear the burka, a garment that covered their entire bodies, including a gauze panel over the eyes.

They would have been happier for her to wear the Pakistani shalwar kameez and a loose headscarf. "But I found liberation in Islam. It gave me the confidence to insist on a good education and reject the arranged marriage. Islam made sense to me, and I could understand it, as opposed to what I had grown up with. Plus, it was compatible with being British—being a British Muslim, rather than Pakistani."

Shagufta was influenced by her friend Soraya's decision to put on hijab. Soraya's French Catholic/Muslim liberal background could not have been more different but, like Shagufta, she found in the Koran an affirmation of herself as a woman: "The Koran says that men and women are equal in the eyes of God, and that we are like a garment for each other to protect one another."

The equality and complementarity of the sexes

Again and again, the women emphasise these two themes, evoked in richly poetic Koranic metaphor: first, the equality of the sexes in the eyes of God (the most meaningful equality of all, they argue), and second, the complementarity of the sexes. As the Koran puts it, "I created you from one soul, and from that soul I created its mate so that you may live in harmony and love."

It is true that there is plenty of material in the Koran that is more egalitarian than the western Christian tradition, which was heavily influenced by the misogyny of Greek thought. Perhaps the most fundamental is that the Islamic God does not have a gender. Arabic may refer to him by use of the male pronoun, but he is never described as "father" or "lord" as he is in the Judaeo-Christian tradition. Indeed, the Islamic God has characteristics that are expressly feminine; one of his most important "names" is al-Rahman (the All-Compassionate) from the Arabic rahma, which comes from the word rahim, meaning womb. In Islamic mysticism, the divinely beloved is female, unlike in Christian mysticism—for example, Bernini's famous statue in Rome of St Teresa of Avila is in love with the male Christ. As one Muslim woman, Sartaz Aziz, writes, "I am deeply grateful that my first ideas of God were formed by Islam, because I was able to think of the Highest Power as one without sex or race and thus completely unpatriarchal."

Jasmin also escaped from an arranged marriage by discovering Islam. Her transition to full religious observance came after university, when she was working for a television company. "I went to Agadir on holiday, returned with a fantastic tan, but went back to work in a hijab. One week in a skimpy swimsuit, the next in a hijab. One of my colleagues couldn't understand. She was crying as she said to me, "One moment you were a sex kitten, the next you're all wrapped up. She thought I was repressing myself; I felt I had achieved liberation.

"The attention I got from the other sex changed. Instead of a sexual approach, they had to take an interest in what was in my head and in my personality, rather than my body. Sometimes, when I flick through a fashion magazine, I think of taking off the hijab, but it passes quickly. Too many women exert power through their sexuality, and that's degrading to women. It's a form of enslavement."

Hijab and sexuality

The importance of each of these women's decisions to wear the hijab leads quickly to a heated discussion about where and how and why one expresses one's sexuality. All the women agree that this is one of the biggest sources of misunderstanding between western feminists and Muslim women. They do not wish to express their sexuality in public, and believe that its proper place is in the privacy of an intimate relationship. Sexuality is not to be used to assert power but to express love, they add. What they hotly deny is that veiling, and modesty in public, is a form of repression. It is not about shame of the female body, as western feminists sometimes insist, but about claiming privacy over their bodies. The Moroccan writer, Fatima Mernissi, ponders on how, in the west, women reclaiming their bodies has led to the public expression of their sexuality, whereas in Islam it is about modesty. The associations with shame and repression stem from the influence of the Christian tradition's hostility to sexuality and hence women, and the legacy of confusion and guilt that has bequeathed western society. Islam, on the other hand, has a healthy honesty and acceptance of human sexuality, which is evident in a wealth of detail in Islamic jurisprudence, they argue.

Dr Tim Winter, a Muslim convert and Cambridge lecturer, probably one of the most respected Islamic scholars in Britain, corroborates the assertion that Islam does not accept the mythology of Eve seducing Adam, and thus triggering the Fall and the endless cycle of death and procreation. According to

Christian thought, sex was the result of human beings' fallen state and was traditionally regarded with distaste; celibacy was promoted as a sublimation of sexual energies in pursuit of God, epitomised by Christ's celibate life.

> *There is plenty of material in the Koran that is more egalitarian than the western Christian tradition, which was heavily influenced by the misogyny of Greek thought.*

Nothing provides a sharper contrast with that model of holiness than the life of the Prophet Mohammed, who took 12 wives after the death of his first wife, Khadija. His love for his wives and sexual relationships with them are referred to in the hadith (the sayings of the Prophet). One reference even extols the Prophet's virility, revealing how he could visit all of his wives in one night. This, says Dr Winter, makes him a full, complete man, closer to models of holiness such as Krishna or a Jewish patriarch such as King Solomon with his many wives.

Indeed, one of the injunctions on a husband is that he must sexually satisfy his wife; the Prophet recommends foreplay, and a great Islamic scholar, Imam Ghazali, warned men not to come too quickly. As Mernissi points out in *Beyond The Veil*, Islam always understood that women's sexuality was active, while western Christianity socialised women into accepting sexual passivity—the "lie back and think of England" approach. The latter, argues Mernissi, was a way of internalising in women the control on female sexuality that men wanted; Muslim cultures used external controls of segregation and male authority.

Affirmation of women's sexuality

Back at ArRum, the women say that, for them, the affirmation of women's sexuality in Islam renders pointless many of the battles fought by western feminists. They have no need of Madonna-style exhibitionism to assert the power of female sexuality. Indeed, one woman said that the one achievement of feminism that she admired was to break down the restrictive passivity of Victorian perceptions of female sexuality.

Aisha and Khadija come out as the two top Koranic role models for these women, and both are quoted as examples of the prominence of women in the development of Islam. Khadija, the Prophet's first wife, was old (40) by the standards of the day when she proposed to the 25-year-old Mohammed. His first believer, she was his sole wife and a close adviser until her death. It was only then that the Prophet took other wives; he married several older widows, but Aisha was much younger than the Prophet, highly intelligent and assertive. There are several stories of how jealous she was of the Prophet's other wives and of how much he loved her. He died in her arms, and she became one of the first teachers of Islam after his death.

All the women I interviewed roll off a long list of hadiths and Koranic verses to support women's rights: the right to education; the right to work and their right to keep the money they earn, while men must use their earnings to look after their womenfolk; property rights; in one school of Islamic thought, women don't have to clean or cook for their husbands unless they are paid for it (wages for housework long before the 20th century thought it had invented it); the fact that the Prophet, according to Aisha, was something of a new man, and used to clean and sew when he wasn't praying; and then there is the praise lavished on the emotional qualities engendered by motherhood of nurturing and patience, with the Prophet's repeated injunctions to honour your mother.

Western unease with the Koran

But there are other parts of Koranic tradition that, to a western eye, seem deeply shocking. By some accounts, Aisha was only nine when her marriage to the Prophet (who was then in his fifties) was consummated. Or that, although the Koran insists that a man should treat all his wives equally, the Prophet admitted that he had a favourite, Aisha. Or the controversial incident when the Prophet glimpsed the wife of his adopted son and, after she had been divorced, he married her. Worst of all to a sceptical western eye, the Prophet often invoked God to explain such incidents.

This is very sensitive territory for devout Muslim women. For believers, the Prophet's life was perfect and according to God's plan. They haven't the freedom to develop the critical analytical tradition of western feminism, which has been so important in understanding how patriarchy has influenced religious, legal, moral and political systems. So, either they offer long explanations (such as that Aisha's age was due to the custom of the time and was probably not much different from the Virgin Mary's), or they acknowledge there are some things that they find very difficult. As one woman put it, "When I read about the Prophet's life, I feel it is unjust: he favoured one wife over another, and that makes me uneasy. I haven't found a scholar who can explain it, but I believe in a just God and the wisdom of the Prophet, so I take it on trust. That's faith. To have real knowledge of Islam is to study it for a long time; eventually, I might find an interpretation that satisfies me."

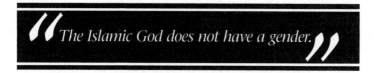

The Islamic God does not have a gender.

These are the sort of explanations that simply fail to convince a sceptical western mind. Perhaps one of the hardest things for a woman to accept in the Koranic tradition is polygamy and, indeed, many of the women I spoke to conceded some unease here. Although some were prepared to consider a polygamous marriage, they all confessed that it would be very difficult; one married woman had even included a prohibition on a second wife in her pre-nuptial contract (a Koranic invention that is mutually negotiated and can cover everything from housework to the frequency of sex). They had various explanations for why the Koran allows men to take four wives, such as the need to provide for war widows in a nomadic warrior culture. With the advent of the welfare state, such arguments are hard to sustain, as several of the women admitted.

Dr Rabia Malik, a psychotherapist, sometimes finds herself in the difficult position of having clients who want to take another wife: "Usually, the first wife doesn't satisfy them intellectually or sexually, and they start to think of taking a second wife, and I try to help them find solutions within their existing relationship."

Both Dr Malik and Humera Khan, founder of the women-run organisation An-Nisa, believe that the Koranic conditions on polygamy are so hard to meet that they virtually rule it out: only those men who can treat their wives equally are allowed more than one. But the fact remains that polygamy, though by no means the norm, is practised in all Muslim countries.

Mernissi believes that this is an explicit humiliation of women, because it asserts that one woman can't satisfy a man; interestingly, Mernissi, a stout critic of certain aspects of Islam, is regarded with some suspicion by many of the women I spoke to.

Dr Winter takes a different tack, defending polygamy by arguing that it is widely practised in the west, from Bill Clinton to Prince Charles. It is, he says, simply more cruel in the west, because all the "wives" bar one are deprived of legal status and dignity. Controversially, he insists that "men are biologically designed to desire a plurality of women . . . and will always do so".

Gender stereotypes

Such gender stereotypes (which are guaranteed to infuriate most western feminists) peppered all my interviews. The Muslim women I spoke to happily talked of women as being "more emotional" and men as "more rational". This was not the result of socialisation, but of nature, and western science was only finally catching up with Koranic insight into the profound differences and complementarity of the sexes. But they denied that this meant that women had to stay at home and men go out to work—they pointed out that many Muslim women work, both in the UK and abroad. The point was that equality did not mean the same in the two cultures, so that the preoccupation in western feminism to achieve and compete on equal terms in the public sphere was a response to the west's own history of seeing women as inferior. What the vast majority of women really want to do is to have and care for children, they said, and a genuinely equal society would be the one that honours that role and provides them with the financial resources to concentrate on it. After such responsibilities have been met (and, with the extended family, there are many to help with childcare), the woman is free to work. To Muslim women, equality means giving their femininity equal worth in the purpose of every human life—to know God. That's as possible in the domestic life of home and children as it is in the marketplace.

As Humera points out, Islam is a home-centred, family-oriented religion that, given the central role of women in both, explains the power of women in Muslim society. Part of the reason why westerners often don't grasp this, explains Dr Winter, is because this home life is private. Muslim cities don't have the grand civic spaces of European cities; they have little alleyways and the vibrant family life takes place behind high walls. The debate about the balance between the private and the public sphere has become much more acute, he says, with the development of industrialisation and the men leaving the home to work long hours. Dr Winter is sharply critical of the west's resolution of the balance between private family life and public life, arguing that the home has almost become a dormitory where the exhausted two-career couple meet briefly, rather than a setting in which children and the elderly can thrive, and where there is a range of familial relationships.

The way in which the traditional segregation is breaking down is one of the most problematic issues in current Islamic thinking. Dr Winter believes that some form of segregation would benefit women in the way that single-sex schooling helps girls develop more confidence, and would help prevent the problems of marriage breakdown experienced in the west: "Segregation has proved a spur in Iran to employing more women, for example," he says. "They now have quotas in the universities so women can be taught by women." But he goes on to acknowledge that "the practice of early Islam did not mean strict segregation, and the historic record is of a more relaxed and open society".

> **//** *One of the injunctions on a husband is that he must sexually satisfy his wife.* **//**

Many Muslims argue that the Prophet's injunction that no one address his wives except through a veil is the model for relations between the sexes. Strict segregation with women confined to the private sphere has been the rule in most Muslim cultures, though rarely as extreme as under the Taliban in Afghanistan. Dr Winter admits that total segregation in the workplace is not practicable, so that leaves devout Muslims with a dilemma of balancing the woman's right to work and be educated with the need to keep to Koranic tradition. The women I met at ArRum all live with their families or relatives, yet they work in mixed environments and travel to attend study courses (they claim they are allowed to travel more than 50 miles from home without a male companion if they are studying Islam). They say they naturally prefer a degree of segregation, enjoying deeper female friendships, rather than the confusing ambiguities of friendships with men. But the result is intense pressure on the women themselves.

Oppressive traditions are un-Islamic

All the women I spoke to, without a moment's hesitation, dismiss the restrictions in the many Islamic countries that oppress women as unIslamic "cultural practices", for example women not being allowed to drive or travel alone in Saudi Arabia. Blaming Islam for practices such as female circumcision, they claim, is the equivalent of blaming feminism for domestic violence—it is linking totally unrelated phenomena. Again, the absence of a critical analysis of the tradition is striking, and there is no answer to the question of why, if Islam offers women a bill of rights, it has not liberated more women. The point, they reply, is that male chauvinism and its bid to control women exists the world over; it simply takes different forms, and when women are educated and know what Islam really means, they can fight back.

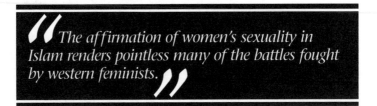

The affirmation of women's sexuality in Islam renders pointless many of the battles fought by western feminists.

They refuse to accept that some of the provisions of Sharia law seem to institutionalise inequality, such as the rule that a woman's evidence must be backed up by another woman. Shagufta admitted that she could see how an outsider might find the idea of stoning adulterers to death, the punishment prescribed in Sharia, as horrific, but, as her friends quickly pointed out, it requires four witnesses to the act of sexual penetration to convict an adulterer—a standard of proof so exacting, they claim, that it would be virtually impossible to achieve.

What women such as Shagufta, Maha, Soraya, Fareena and Jasmin want is to return to the freedoms that Islam brought women in the 7th century and beyond, when women became prominent Islamic scholars, poets and thinkers. "We need a reformation in this global community," said Fareena. "We need to go back to the Islam of the golden age from the 7th to the

13th century." Soraya recognises that this desire to return to the 7th century is paradoxically close to the avowed aims of the Taliban and other fundamentalist groups, but the struggle is over interpretations of what is the true Islam, and British Muslim women are all too well aware of how fragile their position is, defending themselves against criticism from all sides— both from the westerners who accuse them of being oppressed and from the traditional Muslim cultures shocked by their independence and "westernisation".

Danger of backlash

The biggest danger is of a backlash in which the position of women is politicised as it was under the Taliban, where women were not allowed to work or be educated. In such a context, Dr Winter says, women are repressed to salve the sense of Islamic pride wounded by western hegemony and the savage poverty of many Muslim countries. Women are the traditional symbol of honour, and find themselves subjected to restrictions to safeguard their (and the next generation's) contamination from western culture.

So there is a striking bravery in these British Muslim women in their struggle to understand what they see as timeless truths and apply them to 21st-century life. They assiduously attend home-study circles, travel to California and the Middle East for special courses, take up correspondence courses with Islamic scholars and read to deepen their knowledge of Islam, and they believe they are pioneering a spiritual renewal and a rediscovery of their faith that empowers women.

8

Islamic Restrictions on Turkish Women's Sexual Behavior Violate Their Rights

Pinar Ilkkaracan

Pinar Ilkkaracan, a psychotherapist and researcher, is in private practice in Istanbul, Turkey. She is also the founder and coordinator of Women for Women's Human Rights. Ilkkaracan is the editor of the recently published book Women and Sexuality in Muslim Societies, *a collection of articles by women from throughout the Muslim world.*

Islam's traditional view of women's sexuality is contradictory in that it is portrayed as both a healthy, pleasurable, and natural part of life, as well as a dangerous force that needs to be controlled to prevent social chaos. Interviews with nearly six hundred women in eastern Turkey, a secular state with a mostly Muslim population, revealed that sexual behavior is influenced by religious affiliation as well as tribal customs and economic conditions. The women were questioned on a broad array of topics, including marriage customs, bride prices, polygyny, reproductive health, and domestic violence ranging from marital rape to honor killings. Women who belonged to conservative religious sects reported more violations of their human rights and more severe controls over their sexual behavior than women who belonged to less conservative groups. The international community must work to end this violation of woman's rights.

Pinar Ilkkaracan, *Good Sex: Feminist Perspectives from the World's Religions*, edited by Patricia B. Jung and Radhika Balakrishnan. Piscataway, NJ: Rutgers University Press, 2001. Copyright © 2001 by Pinar Ilkkaracan. Reproduced by permission.

The control over women's sexuality through restriction, coercion, violence or more complicated forms of political and social manipulation remains the most powerful tool of patriarchy in the majority of societies. Religion is often misused, both as an instrument of this control mechanism and as a cultural system, to legitimize the violation of women's human rights. However, concentrating on the role of religion in constructing women's sexuality without taking into consideration its interaction with the economic and political structures in a particular community can lead to erroneous conclusions.

Like many other religions, Islam does not have a static or monolithic tradition. Islam has interacted with sociopolitical and economic conditions at a particular time and geographic location in order to ensure its survival and power. In the process, it has not only absorbed the practices and traditions of the two other monotheistic religions born in the same territory, namely Judaism and Christianity, but also the pre-Islamic practices and traditions of the particular geographic location in which it has striven to survive and gain power as a cultural and political system. Thus, it is very difficult to define what is intrinsic to Islam in organizing sexual behavior. The issue becomes even more complicated when we look at the interaction of factors such as class and race with Islam at a particular time and place, which has led to different religious interpretations and practices. All of these factors often produce different schools of Islamic thought, some of which can exist even within the same community.

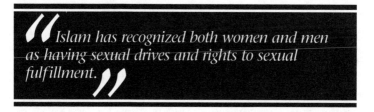

Islam has recognized both women and men as having sexual drives and rights to sexual fulfillment.

Discourses on sexuality in Islam often fail to consider differences in practices in different Muslim communities as well as the spaces of negotiability created by social taboos and silences related to sexual behavior. Nonetheless, even discourses based on an analysis of the Koran and the literature traditionally accepted as establishing the normative practices of Islam can lead to contradictory conclusions about the construction of women's sexuality. On the one hand, Islam has recognized both women and men as having sexual drives and rights to sexual fulfillment. Eroticism is presented as a good in itself, both a foretaste of heaven and on earth a divinely ordained necessity for reproduction. Women, like men, are believed to experience orgasms. On the other hand, particularly in terms of sexual drives, males and females are construed as opposites, men as rational and capable of self control; women as emotional and lacking self-control. Female sexuality, if uncontrolled, is portrayed as leading to social chaos (*fitna*). Social order thus requires male control of women's bodies and sexuality. However, the specific patriarchal mechanisms that are utilized to maintain this control differ according to geographical location, time, class and race and depend on the economic and political realities of a given community.

> *Female sexuality, if uncontrolled, is portrayed as leading to social chaos.*

The historical role of the interaction of Islam with specific socioeconomic and political systems in shaping women's sexuality in different Muslim communities is still a relatively unexplored issue. Although the 1990's witnessed a spurt of new research on women's history and gender organization in Muslim societies, the accumulated knowledge is still too rudimentary to throw light on such a complex and sensitive issue as women's sexuality. Even in recent decades, women's own accounts on the issue have remained very rare. In most Muslim societies there is a striking lack of empirical data on sexual behavior, especially women's.

In such a context, research on the official, religious and customary laws and practices that determine the organization of gender and the context of women's sexuality in different Muslim societies could throw light on the ways religion is used to create and perpetuate the oppression and injustice women experience in these societies. It would also play an invaluable role in deconstructing the myth of a uniform Islam, which fundamentalists claim consists of "a divine and eternal truth.". . .

This [selection] examines laws and practices related to important elements in shaping the context of women's sexuality: civil versus religious marriages, bride prices, polygyny, women's consent to marriage, reproductive health, the possible consequences of extramarital relationships for women, and domestic violence. The analysis is based on interviews conducted with 599 women in eastern Turkey.

Historical forces in Turkey

Turkey, which is a predominantly Muslim country, is the heir of the Ottoman Empire in which the Koran formed the basis of family law. Turkey was founded as a republic in 1923 as a result of the victory of reformists over foreign occupying armies as well as over conservative forces at home. The foundation of the republic was followed by the introduction of several revolutionary changes for women. Turkey is unique in the Muslim world in the extent of its secular, progressive reforms of the family code affecting women's lives. In 1926, the introduction of the Turkish Civil Code, which is based on the Swiss Civil Code, banned polygamy and granted women equal rights in matters of divorce, child custody and inheritance. Yet, even several decades after these reforms, customary and religious laws and practices that often breach official laws are used as tools to control women's sexuality and maintain the imbalance of power in sexual relations. This is especially the case for women living in eastern Turkey, which can at best be characterized as a semi-feudal, traditional, agricultural economy. The situation of many women living in the region has worsened as a result of the armed conflict since 1984 between the Turkish security forces and the separatist Kurdistan Worker's Party (PKK). . . .

Socioeconomic disparities

Turkey is one of the countries suffering from problems resulting from regional disparities in socioeconomic conditions. The unfavorable effects of these disparities are experienced more by women than men. Western Turkey consumes most available resources and is also highly urbanized, while in the eastern section most of the population lives in rural areas. Although primary school education has been mandatory in Turkey since 1927, in 1990 half of the women in eastern Turkey were illiterate, compared with 21.6 percent of the men. The illiteracy rates are much lower in western Turkey, at 19.7 and 7.4 percent for women and men, respectively. As a consequence of the armed conflict, the number and quality of the educational institutions in the region is declining, limiting still further women's educational opportunities. Regional differences in women's participation in the labor force participation are also striking. In the west, the proportion of women working for pay is 40 percent, while in the east approximately 90 percent of women are still unpaid family workers. . . .

Fertility and contraception

The eastern region has the highest fertility rate in the country. In 1992, the fertility rate in the region there was 4.4 compared with 2.0 in the western region and 2.7 in Turkey as a whole. Some of the reasons behind the desire for a high number of children in the region are the aspiration for a powerful tribe, family elders' expectations of a boy child, and the belief that Allah will provide food for each person. Approximately 11 percent of women living in the east have their first child between fifteen to nineteen years of age, compared to 8.3 percent in the west. The level of current use of contraception is only 42 percent in the east, whereas it exceeds 70 percent in the west and 60 percent in other regions of Turkey. When asked about the total number of their children, mothers often mention only the number of sons, omitting their daughters, as girls do not count. The situation has worsened as women's bodies have become the sites of the conflict between the Turkish security forces and PKK. The Turkish state is interested in reducing the fertility rate in order to increase its economic and political domination of the region, whereas the PKK propagandizes against contraception of all kinds, which they define as "a tool of the state to eradicate the Kurdish folk".

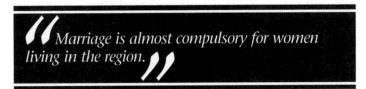

Marriage is almost compulsory for women living in the region.

Marriage is almost compulsory for women living in the region. Of the respondents who were over twenty-four years of age, 97 percent were or had been married, as had all of the women who were over thirty-four years of age. Only a small percentage (0.6 percent) were divorced, indicating the rarity of marital dissolution in the region. . . .

As it is practiced in eastern Turkey, the payment of a bride price—the sum given by the husband or husband's family to the bride's kinsmen for the realization of marriage—symbolizes men's control over a woman and over the transfer of her productive and reproductive capacities to her husband's kin group. This tradition is widespread in the region and plays an important role in the attitude of men, who assume that through this payment they have gained all rights over their wives' sexuality and fertility. Sixty-one percent of women indicated that their husbands had to pay a bride price for them. In fact, this tradition of families selling women for marriage remains prevalent despite the fact that more than three-quarters of the women (78.9 percent) indicated that they were against the tradition. More than half of the women (56.3 percent) responded to an open-ended question about the reasons for opposing the bride price by saying "because women/human beings are not a commodity to be sold". It is interesting to note that at least one-fifth (21.4 percent) of the respondents stated that the main reason they were against the bride price was that they considered the tradition to be "against Islam" or "a sin". On the other hand, none of the women who supported bride price saw it as a religious practice. Thus, the bride price constitutes a clear example of a patriarchal custom practiced even if it is perceived to be incompatible with religious laws.

Polygyny and forced marriages

In the Muslim world, the opinions of religious thinkers on both polygamy and practices related to it differ widely. Some believe that Islam does not allow polygamy, basing their arguments on Koranic verses Surah an-Nisa, which forbids polygyny unless the husband treats his wives equally and does not differentiate in the slightest degree between them. Nonetheless, polygyny has become an established part of traditional religious law and practice in many Muslim countries. Polygamy has been banned in Turkey since 1926. As a result, in polygynous marriages, only one wife can have a civil marriage; the others can have only religious marriages. This situation immediately creates inequality between the wives as only one of them has access to legally binding rights under the Civil Code, such as rights related to divorce, maintenance, inheritance or custody. . . .

Under the Turkish Civil Code, the consent of both the woman and the man is a precondition for marriage, yet women living in the region often have no influence over the choice of their prospective partner and are frequently married against their will. In fact, even in cases in which women are consulted about the choice of a husband, they cannot exercise their right of consent to the full because of a high degree of social control over women's sexuality maintained by the taboo on premarital sex, the practice of endogamy, or the threat of violence against women who do not comply with the choice of the family.

> *The bride price constitutes a clear example of a patriarchal custom practiced even if it is perceived to be incompatible with religious laws.*

Most of the marriages (61.4 percent) were arranged by the family and only one in four marriages was arranged by the couple themselves. Although the percentage of married Alevi[1] women who had arranged their marriages autonomously was well above the average, the majority of Alevi marriages were also arranged marriages. Even when the marriage is arranged by the couple, the agreement of their families is very often a precondition to it. Every twentieth marriage was a *berdel* case, a tradition in which a woman is offered as compensation to the family of her father's or brother's wife. These marriages are based on the exchange of brides that have "equal value", which means that if one marriage fails, the other has to fail too. In such marriages, the women are more or less hostages. Families are not likely to allow them to run away or divorce. . .

More than half of the women (50.8 percent) were married without their consent and 45.7 percent were not even consulted about their partner or the marriage. Those who had not met the husband before the marriage constituted 51.6 percent of the participants. . . .

Reproductive rights

There are no legal restrictions on contraception in Turkey, and family planning is increasingly encouraged by the state. Family planning seems to be acceptable in many Muslim countries

1. followers of a different tradition from the majority of Islamic worshippers

and societies, especially when economic conditions require it.
Since 1983, abortion has been legal until the end of the tenth
week of pregnancy. However, in eastern Turkey, as in the rest of
the country, contraception, like childbearing, is considered to
be applicable only to married women, as sex or childbirth is a
taboo issue for the most unmarried women. As a result, many
women have no chance of receiving any information about
contraception before marriage. . . .

Honor killings

At present, neither the Turkish Civil Code nor the Turkish
Criminal Code differentiate between men and women on the
issue of fornication. Proof of fornication entitles the injured
party to file for divorce on the grounds of infidelity, which can
be proved by any means (e.g. witnesses) and enables the injured party to claim damages. However, extramarital relationships are an absolute social taboo for women living in eastern
Turkey, whereas men's extramarital affairs are widely accepted
and even socially legalized in many cases through the institution of polygyny. The majority of women interviewed (66.6
percent) believed that, contrary to the law, even if they wanted
to, they could not divorce a husband who committed adultery.
Although an increase in women's educational levels increases
women's openness to the possibility of divorce, 31.5 percent of
women who had secondary or higher education still believed
that they could not divorce their husbands on the grounds of
adultery. There was no difference in the perception of possible
divorce between women living in urban and rural areas. . . .

In contrast to many men who can practice adultery without fear of divorce by their wives, even though such divorce is
allowed by the Civil Code, the customary penalty in the region
for women suspected of this offense is death. These so-called
honor killings are one of the most dreadful examples of collec-
tive control of women's sexuality. *Honor killing* is a term used to
describe the murder of a woman suspected of having trans-
gressed the limits on sexual behavior as imposed by tradition,
specifically, engaging in a premarital relationship with the opposite sex or in a suspected extramarital affair. The use of the
word *honor* in relation to the crime of murder is reflective of a
culture where men define their personal and family honor
through the sexual behavior of their women kin. This custom
is in sharp contradiction to the official law. Since June 1998,

fornication, either by women or men, has not been defined as even a criminal offense in Turkey. Thus, there are no official laws in Turkey restricting the right of a woman to engage in a relationship with any man or woman of her choice before, during or after marriage.

Only 27.5 percent of the respondents believed that the possible reaction of their husbands towards an extramarital affair of theirs would be divorce. The majority (66.6 percent) thought that their husbands would kill them if they suspected them of an extramarital affair. This percentage was higher among those who had little or no education, those who had only a religious marriage, and those who lived in rural areas. . . .

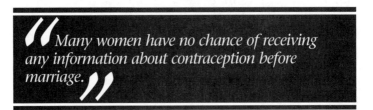

Many women have no chance of receiving any information about contraception before marriage.

The practice of honor killings is not based on the Koran. Although the Koran forbids adultery and foresees heavy punishment (one hundred lashes) for both women and men guilty of adultery or fornication; it requires four witnesses to the act. Otherwise, if a woman denies the accusation, then it is her word that must be accepted rather than that of her accusing husband. The Koran states that not only should evidence of men who accuse women of being adulterous without producing at least four witnesses be rejected, but also that they should be punished by eighty lashes as they are deemed to be "wicked transgressors". However, 46.3 percent of women who feared being killed if they committed adultery stated that the only customary proof required for an honor killing was the husband's claim to have seen it with his own eyes; the women often added that they perceive this practice as the utmost injustice. They noted that even if the husband was lying, he would be believed by the community, as a man's word is generally accepted to be true. Only 18.6 percent stated that the husband had to have witnesses to the act, while 27.3 percent said that he needed to prove it in some other way.

Although no provision in the Turkish Criminal Code explicitly refers to "crimes of honor", the tradition of honor killing is supported by the law that considers an extramarital affair involving a husband or wife to be a "provocation" and reduces the sentence by one-eighth if such provocation is considered to have taken place. In most cases, in order to escape sentences required for murder under the Turkish Criminal Code, the so-called family council does not hesitate to order a male child in the family to commit the murder. Such a youth would be expected to receive a lighter punishment, based on the law that a sentence is reduced by one-third if the crime is committed by someone who is considered by law to be a minor. In such situations, the members of the family council— male relatives of the woman who have actually decided and planned the murder—receive no punishment. The lack of legal recognition of honor crimes is a severe violation of women's basic human rights. The feudal structure and the absence of a local women's movement in the region are serious impediments in the fight against honor killings.

Violence

More than half of all married women living in the region stated that they were subjected to physical, emotional and verbal violence by their husbands (57.9 percent, 56.6 percent and 76.7 percent, respectively). Those who were subjected to sexual violence (marital rape) constituted 51.9 percent of the participants. As the educational level of women and their husbands increases, the extent of domestic violence declines but by no means disappears. One-third of women who had a secondary or higher education were subjected to emotional and physical violence by their husbands, and one-quarter indicated that they had experienced marital rape. The extent of domestic violence experienced by women, including marital rape, not only negatively affects women's sexual health and their perception of sexuality but also reduces their chances of creating and applying strategies against the violation of their rights. . . .

Injustices in the name of Islam

The research findings detailed here all reflect a number of control mechanisms on women's sexuality in eastern Turkey, economically the least developed region of the country, where semifeudal structures still dictate both the organization of gender and sexual relations for the majority of women. The social pressure on women to marry early, forced and arranged marriages, the tradition of bride money, the extended exchange of wives between families, and the extent of the threat of violence against women who transgress the limits on sexual behavior as imposed by traditions constitute some of the control mechanisms which are supported by customary and religious practices in the region. . . . Research findings also indicate that education is often one of the most important tools for women in countering the violation of their human rights.

As in many other countries, most women in the region are not aware of their rights, and there are no services to which they have access to learn about them. The expansion of such services for women is one of the main preconditions for their creating strategies to defend their rights. . . .

To raise public awareness of, and to create preventive strategies against these practices, it is essential to identify and integrate them into the women's human rights agenda on the national and international levels. This is a crucial step in the fight against conservative and fundamentalist politics aimed at stifling the debate on the violation of women's human rights through practices deemed "Islamic." As [scholar] Riffat Hassan asserts, the most important task for Muslims today lies in making peace, "provided they understand that peace is a dynamic state predicted on the idea of justice for all, and justice not only in the legal sense but also in the socio-economic, political and personal sense, i.e., justice between man and man and—what is perhaps even more important—justice between man and woman."

9

Polygamy Benefits Islamic Women

Abu Ameenah Bilal Philips

Abu Ameenah Bilal Philips is a lecturer in Arabic and Islamic studies at the American University in Dubai and Ajman University in Ajman, United Arab Emirates.

Polygamy is a practice in which a spouse of either sex may have more than one mate at the same time. In contrast, in the practice of polygyny, only the males may have more than one mate. Polygyny has been practiced for thousands of years by Muslim societies. Only recently have non-Muslims attacked Islamic institutions of marriage and polygyny. Those critics wrongly argue that monogamy is a superior practice. The Western women suffer because they do not have the socioeconomic protections that polygynous Muslim society offers Islamic women. Although polygny may be painful for some women, Muslims must accept the practice that Allah decreed.

This article is not put together in defense of polygyny (plural marriage) for Allah has already confirmed its validity as clearly stated in the Noble Quran:

> Marry of the women that please you, two, three or four, but if you fear that you will not be able to deal justly with them, then only one.

Moreover, the Prophet (pbuh)[1] demonstrated in detail how

---

1. praise be upon him; a phrase of respect used after the Prophet's name

polygyny should be put into practice by his divinely guided lifestyle.

Polygyny was the practise of most of the major companions of the Prophet (pbuh) as well as many outstanding Muslim scholars from the earliest time of Islam up to the present. Polygyny was also practised among a portion of the general masses in most Muslim countries before and after the advent of European colonization.

In fact, it is only in recent times (early twentieth century) that a loud new cry has been raised by non-Muslims attacking the institution of marriage in Islam due to its recognition of polygyny and the ease with which divorce may be obtained. They propose the replacement of the Islamic form of marriage with restrictive impractical monogamy practised in the West, arguing that it is the only just and civilized form of marriage. However, to this day, polygyny continues to be practised by some Muslims throughout the Muslim world.

Christian monogamy did not civilize the world

Having said that, however, there are a few points raised by the opponents of Islam which should be answered. Firstly, among these is the totally erroneous claim that Christianity's introduction of monogamy not only protected the rights of women but also had a civilizing effect on the world in the realm of human relations. First of all, it should be noted that there are no scriptural accounts of Jesus prohibiting polygyny, and early Christians were polygynous, following Jewish tradition. Some of the Church Fathers accused the Jewish rabbis of sensuality, yet not a single church council in the early centuries opposed polygyny nor was any obstacle placed in the way of its practice. In fact, St. Augustine declared openly that he did not condemn it. [German reformer Martin] Luther, on occasion, spoke of it with considerable toleration and was known to have approved the bigamous status of [German nobleman] Philip of Hesse. In 1531, the Anabaptists openly preached that a true Christian must have several wives. There was even a time in 1650 when some of the Christian leaders resolved that every man should be allowed to marry two women. It is also recorded that the German reformers, even as late as the sixteenth century, admitted the validity of a second and third marriage contemporaneously with the first in default of issue and other similar causes. In fact, it was only after Christianity was revised according to Paulian doctrines that concepts of monogamy were introduced into Christian philosophy in order for it to conform to Greco-Roman culture. Greece and Rome had evolved an institutionalized form of monogamy in societies where the majority of the population were slave women who could be used freely for sexual purposes. Hence what was termed monogamy in theory was in fact unrestricted polygamy.

Christianity despised women

Secondly, along with the development of monasticism there arose a philosophy which regarded every gratification of the sexual impulse with suspicion and disgust. For those who chose celibacy or self-denial as their way of life, the greatest challenge was their own sexual desires. The writings of early monks are filled with their descriptions of dreams in which they are tormented by beautiful and alluring women. Many Christian saints were reported to have been convinced that they were tempted at night by voluptuous and lascivious female demons called succubi that tormented them. While nuns and other Christian women, on the other hand, asserted that they were visited at night by equally alluring beings called incubi who had sex with them. Women were despised and blamed for corruption based on Eve's supposed submission to the Devil and her subsequent encouragement to Adam to eat from the forbidden tree. Some Christian scholars of the past even interpreted the forbidden tree as sex itself. The following are statements of canonized saints of Christianity concerning women: "Woman is the daughter of falsehood, a sentinel of Hell, the enemy of peace; through her Adam lost paradise (St. John Damascene)". "Woman is the arm of the Devil, her voice is the hissing of the serpent (St. Anthony)". "Woman has the poison of an asp, the malice of a dragon (St. Gregory the Great)". Hence, sex was looked upon as an evil impulse necessary for procreation but despised for pleasure. And, the acceptable form of marriage was reduced to the simplest possible terms, monogamy.

Monogamy protects the male's right to play around

The question remains why a male-dominated society should be so opposed to polygyny when such a large number of its married members practise a form of it by engaging in illicit or casual relationships. Some males self-righteously assert that monogamy is maintained to protect the rights of women. But, since when has the Western male been concerned about women's rights? Western society is riddled through and through with socio-economic practices which oppressed women and led to the upsurge of women's liberation movements in recent years, from suffragettes of the early nineteen hundreds to those of recent times.

The reality is that monogamy protects the male's right to play around without any responsibility, since the incidence of infidelity among them is usually much higher than among females. The birth control pills and easy access to abortions opened the door to illicit sex and the female became tempted to join in the fun. Inspite of her natural and general inclination towards meaningful relationships, she became caught up in the so-called sexual revolution. However, she is still the one who suffers from the side effects of the pill, coil and the loop or the trauma of abortion in much the same way as she suffered in the past the shame of child birth out of wedlock. Meanwhile the male continues to enjoy himself worry free, aside from the recent plagues of venereal disease, herpes and A.I.D.S., which are now causing many to reassess their sexual habits. Males in general continue to be protected by monogamy, while prostitutes, call girls, mistresses, secretaries, models, actresses, store clerks, waitresses and girl friends remain their playground.

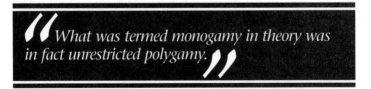

What was termed monogamy in theory was in fact unrestricted polygamy.

The fact is that polygyny is vehemently opposed by male-dominated Western society because it would force men to fidelity. It would encourage them to take socio-economic responsibility for the fulfillment of their polygynous desires and provide protection for the weaker members of society, women and children from mental and physical abuse.

Some might argue that if the stigma of illegitimacy were removed, the problem could be solved without having to resort to the legalization of polygyny. However, every child has a natural desire to know its parents and the resulting chaos in ancestry could easily lead to incestuous relationships.

Females have a vested interest in institutional polygyny because of the obvious socio-economic protection it provides. For the preponderance of females in the world is an established fact. The death-rate at birth is much higher for boys, and women as a whole live longer than men; not to mention the large numbers of men who die daily in the various wars around the world. Thus, although the ratio may vary from country to country the results are still the same; women outnumber men.

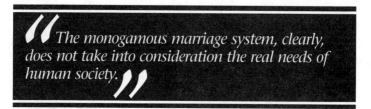

The monogamous marriage system, clearly, does not take into consideration the real needs of human society.

This apparent imbalance has been further aggravated by the fact that homosexuality appears to be more frequent among men than among women. Hence there are more females competing for a diminishing number of males. Consequently, there will always remain a large segment of women unable to fulfill their sexual and psychological needs through legitimate means in monogamous societies. Their presence in an increasingly permissive society also contributes to the break down of Western family structure. A strong family structure is an absolute requirement for a strong and a healthy society. The only way that the family can remain strong and responsive to the needs of its male and female members is through the Islamic form of marriage of which polygyny is a part.

The monogamous marriage system, clearly, does not take into consideration the real needs of human society. It limits possibilities for both men and women while claiming to protect the latter. Instead of providing protection for women, it provides a hypocritical shield for men to hide behind while favoring a wife to the detriment of a girl friend or vice versa. Islam has a complete marriage system which takes into account all the human variables and provides men and women with viable options. To deny the validity and legality of polygyny is tantamount to denying the comprehensiveness of the Islamic marriage system and the wisdom of the divine decree. It is not possible that everything in life should happen according to our feelings and desires. Nor is it possible to live without experiencing pain. On the contrary, Allah has stated in the Noble Quran that Muslims shall be tested:

> Be sure that We shall test you with something of fear and hunger, some loss in goods or lives or the fruits (of your labor), but give glad tidings to those who are patient.

> Do men think that they will be left alone on saying, "We believe", and that they will not be tested?

Neither tests nor pain, whether physical or emotional, can be avoided in this life. Nor can any aspect of the Islamic system be negated merely to justify a particular individual's or group's opinions. Although polygyny may be painful for some women, it is beneficial for other women and for society as a whole. Muslims must accept the whole of Allah's message and submit to the fact that Allah's wisdom is superior to our opinions.

10

Islamic Teachings Uphold Monogamy as the Ideal State of Marriage

Zainah Anwar

Zainah Anwar is the executive director of Sisters in Islam, a nongovernmental organization that is committed to promoting the rights of women within the framework of Islam.

Muslim women have a right to interpret Islamic law and challenge fundamentalists who use the religion to justify inferior treatment of women. Men have promoted biased interpretations of many verses in the Koran, including those about polygamy. They focus on the phrase stating that men may have up to four wives while ignoring the rest of the verse arguing that polygamy is a responsibility that should only be permitted in exceptional circumstances. In fact, the Koran shows that monogamy is the ideal state of Islamic marriage. When women interpret the text, they discover such messages and meanings that traditional education stridently ignores.

The Islamic resurgence that has engulfed most Muslim countries today has thrown forth different levels of tension and competing ideologies within these societies: what Islam, whose Islam is the right Islam? Very often, it is the status and rights of women that have become the first casualty in this battleground.

The struggle for equality and justice for Muslim women

must therefore be placed within the context of women living in Muslim societies where Islam is increasingly shaping and re-defining our lives. Since the early 1970s, Muslim societies in all parts of the world have been caught up in the throes of a resurgent Islam. However, all too often, in the turn to Islam as a way of life and the source for solutions to the ills and injustices that beset our societies, it seems that the place of women has become the first (and easiest) measure of a group's or society's commitment to the faith.

> *We feel strongly we have a right to reclaim our religion . . . in ways that take into consideration the realities and experience of women's lives today.*

It is therefore not surprising that in many Muslim countries today, women's groups are at the forefront in challenging traditional authority and fundamentalists and their use of religion to justify women's subordination and inferior status, and most perniciously, to use religion to silence any dissent or defame or incite hatred against those who offer alternative views or protect and promote the rights of women.

Rejection of belief not possible

For most Muslim women, rejecting religion is not an option. We are believers, and as believers we want to find liberation, truth and justice from within our own faith. We feel strongly we have a right to reclaim our religion, to redefine it, to participate and contribute to an understanding of Islam, how it is codified and implemented—in ways that take into consideration the realities and experience of women's lives today.

Today's Muslim women in a country like Malaysia that is fast modernising and industrialising will no longer accept their inferior status, not even when it is justified in the name of religion. Today's women will not accept that Islam actually promotes injustice and ill-treatment of half the human race. Today's women are challenging the values of patriarchal society where power and authority reside exclusively with the husband, father, brother to whom the wife, daughter and sister owe obedience. For too long, men have defined for us what it is to be a woman, how to be a woman and then to use religion to confine us to these socially constructed limitations that reduce us to being the inferior half of the human race.

Times, however, are achanging. We live in an era where women are educated, travel the world, hold positions of power and responsibility in increasing numbers. Today [2003] in Malaysia, 70 percent of the students enrolled in public sector institutions of higher learning, are girls. The female labour force participation stands at 47 percent and is rising. It can only be expected that women, with increasing knowledge and education, with economic independence, will gain more confidence and courage to speak out in the face of injustice. If the injustice is committed in the name of religion, then today's women will go back to the original source of the religion to find out for themselves whether such a great religion could indeed be so unjust to half of its believers. . . .

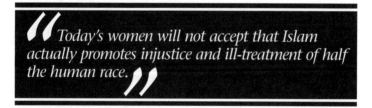

Today's women will not accept that Islam actually promotes injustice and ill-treatment of half the human race.

In the past ten years, more and more progressive scholars have challenged the Islamic agenda of the traditionalist and also the fundamentalist ulama [Islamic scholars] and activists and their intolerance and outright oppression of women. These works which recognise equality between men and women in Islam, which argue for the imperative of ijtihad (reinterpretation of the Qur'an in the context of changing times and circumstances), which address the dynamics between what is universal for all times and what is particular to seventh century Arabia, which look at the socio-historical context of revelation, which articulate the need to differentiate between what is revelation and what is human understanding of the word of God. . . . Such research, methodology, conceptual frameworks developed to deal with the challenge of Islam and modernity have enabled more and more Muslim women activists all over the world to realise the validity and possibility of working within the Islamic framework, that indeed we can find liberation from within Islam. Women have begun to study the Qur'an for themselves and the traditions of the Prophet to better understand Islam and with this knowledge and new found conviction, have begun to stand up to fight for women's right to equality, justice, freedom and dignity within the religious framework.

Our strength comes from our conviction and faith in an Islam that is just, liberating and empowering to us as women. Groups like Sisters in Islam [a nongovernmental organisation based in Malaysia] are reclaiming for ourselves the Islam that liberated women and uplifted our status by giving us rights considered revolutionary 1400 years ago—the right to own, inherit or dispose of our own property, the right to divorce, the right to contract agreements,—all introduced by Islam in the 7th century.

An ethical vision of Islam

It is this ethical vision of the Qur'an that insistently enjoins equality and justice, it is this liberating and revolutionary spirit of Islam that today guides our quest to be treated as fellow human beings of equal worth.

How and why did women's groups like Sisters and individual Muslim scholars, women and men, many of whom have been incredibly generous with their time and scholarship in helping us activists, decide to study the Qur'an and strive to hear the voice of the divine will speaking to our concerns.

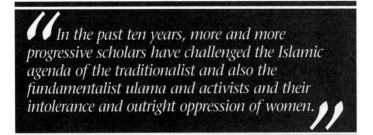

In the past ten years, more and more progressive scholars have challenged the Islamic agenda of the traditionalist and also the fundamentalist ulama and activists and their intolerance and outright oppression of women.

Let me just share with you the process Sisters went through. Like many other women's groups, it is injustice, oppression and ill treatment that mobilised us Muslim women. Sisters in Islam first got together because of our deep concerns over the injustice women suffered under the [Islamic law] syariah system. As professional women and as activists, other women often approached us to confide in us their marital problems and the problems they faced when they approached the religious authorities to seek redress to these problems. We got together first to look into the problems women faced with the implementation of the Islamic Family laws [Malaysian legislation concerning families].

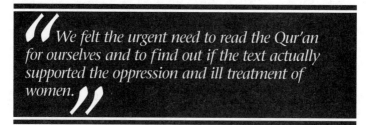

We felt the urgent need to read the Qur'an for ourselves and to find out if the text actually supported the oppression and ill treatment of women.

However, increasingly, we felt that dealing with the law alone was not enough. We felt powerless in the face of complaints by women that they have to suffer in silence because Islam demands that they be obedient to their husbands, because Islam grants their men the right to beat their wives or to take second wives. We felt powerless to hear talks, again and again, in religious classes, over radio and television, in interaction with those in the religious departments and syariah courts where women were often told that men are superior to women, that men have authority over women, that a man has a right to beat his wife, that a woman must obey her husband, the evidence of two women equals one man, the husband has a God-given right to take a second wife, and therefore it is a sin for a woman to deny him that right, that a wife has no right to say no to sex with her husband, that hell is full of women because they leave their heads uncovered and are disobedient to their husbands.

Traditional pronouncements questioned

Where is the justice for women in all these pronouncements? This questioning, and above all, the conviction that Allah could never be unjust, eventually led us to go back to the primary source of our religion, the Qur'an. We felt the urgent need to read the Qur'an for ourselves and to find out if the text actually supported the oppression and ill treatment of women.

This process Sisters went through was the most liberating and spiritually uplifting experience for all of us. We took the path of Iqraq ("Read", the first word revealed to Prophet Muhammad saw) and it opened a world of Islam that we could recognise, a world for women that was filled with love and mercy and with equality and justice. We need not look any further to validate our struggle. Women's rights were rooted in our tradition, in our faith. We were more convinced than ever that it is not Islam that oppresses women, but interpretations of the Qur'an influenced by cultural practices and values of a patriarchal society, which regard women as inferior and subordinate to men.

Men misinterpret the Qur'an

For much of Islamic history, it is men who have interpreted the Qur'an and the traditions for us. The woman's voice, the woman's experience, the woman's realities had been silent and silenced in the reading and interpretation of the text. Thus, when Sisters read the text, we discovered words, messages and meanings that we were never exposed to in all the traditional education on Islam that we went through in our lives.

For us, it was the beginning of a new journey of discovery. It was a revelation to us that the verse on polygamy (Sura an-Nisa, 4:3) explicitly said ". . .if you fear you shall not be able to deal justly with women, then marry only one". How come one half of the verse that said a man can have up to four wives becomes universally known and accepted as a right in Islam and is codified into law, but the other half of the very same verse that promotes monogamy is unheard of . . . until women began to read the Qur'an for ourselves.

Polygamy should be rare

It dawned on us that when men read the verse, they only saw "marry up to four wives." In that phrase, they saw the word of God that validated their desire and their experience. When women read the verse, we clearly saw ". . . if you fear you cannot deal justly with women, then marry only one". Those were the words of Allah that spoke to our fears of injustice. We understood that the right to polygamy was conditional, and if a man cannot fulfil those conditions of equal and just treatment, then Allah said marry only one. In fact the verse goes on to say that ". . . this will be best for you to prevent you from doing injustice". What further validation do we need to argue that polygamy is not an unconditional right in Islam, but is actually a responsibility allowed only in exceptional circumstances.

We did more research on the issue and found out that such interpretation of the verse on polygamy and the Qur'anic view on marriage is actually not something new. It is not the invention of the women's movement in the 20th century. There were many prominent ulama over the centuries and Islamic movements which interpreted that monogamy is the ideal state of marriage in Islam. But their views were marginalised by the ruling elite or the religious establishment. The Qarmatians [an Islamic sect], a movement that challenged Abbasid rule actually banned polygamy among its members and it also banned the institution of concubinage so loved by the ruling elite of the Abbasids.[1]

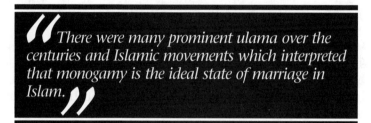

There were many prominent ulama over the centuries and Islamic movements which interpreted that monogamy is the ideal state of marriage in Islam.

In more modern times, renowned Egyptian ulama such as al-Tahtawi and Muhammad Abduh who was Egypt's Grand Mufti at the turn of this century both held the opinion that the Qur'an viewed monogamy as the ideal marriage in Islam. In this century, Abdullah Yusuf Ali, the translator and interpreter of the Qur'an into English that is widely used throughout the world, also held the same view. However, in the new edition of his translated Qur'an, published in 1989 by IIIT [International Institute of Islamic Thought] based in [Herndon, Virginia, near Washington, D.C.], his commentary on the verse on polygamy in which he says that the ideal and original state of marriage in Islam is monogamy, has been deleted by the publishers. Maybe the review committee felt that too many people are reading his version of the Qur'an and are quoting his interpretation to oppose polygamy.

The facts of the Prophet's life are ignored

Those who support polygamy very often say that they are only following the Prophet's way; but they have conveniently ignored the fact that the Prophet married a woman 15 years older than him and he remained monogamous for the first 25

1. rulers of Arabia in the 7th century

years of his marriage, i.e., throughout the life of Siti Khadija, his first wife. It was only after Khadija's death that he married other women, and except for Aisha [the Prophet's favourite wife], the other women were all widows or divorcees and he married them to cement family ties and unite warring tribes.

There is also an authentic hadith [Islamic commentary] (sunan Ibn Majah) which reported that the Prophet objected to his nephew, Saidina Ali Abi Talib who was married to the Prophet's daughter, from taking another wife. He said, Ali could take another wife, only if he divorced Fatimah, the Prophet's daughter ". . . because my daughter is a part of me and what saddens and hurts her, saddens and hurts me too, and any problems that befall her will be felt by me too."

And yet while from young we knew that a Muslim man could have four wives, we did not know that the verse on polygamy actually advocated monogamy, that key Islamic scholars had supported monogamy, that an authentic hadith existed which expressed the Prophet's displeasure that Ali would take another wife and would not allow him to do so without first divorcing his wife. . . .

We need an enlightened interpretation of the Qur'an

If we as believers want to live a life according to the tenets of our faith, a simplistic call to return to an idealised golden age of Islam that have little bearing on the realities of today's world cannot be the answer. And yet the answers can be found within our faith—if only we have the intellectual vigour, the moral courage, and the political will to strive for a more enlightened and progressive interpretation of the Qur'an in our search for answers to deal with our changing times and circumstances. For us in Sisters in Islam, this is not heretical, but an imperative if religion is to be relevant to our lives today.

11

Iranian Women Are Being Sold into Prostitution

Donna M. Hughes

Donna M. Hughes is a professor of women's studies at the University of Rhode Island.

In Iran, girls and women are sold into prostitution with the full knowledge of the country's fundamentalist Islamic rulers. In many cases, even high officials are involved with prostitution rings. Fundamentalists hate women's minds and bodies, and force them to cover themselves with veils. Selling girls and women into prostitution is just another way to dehumanize them. The only way to free them from slavery is to end the Iranian regime.

A measure of Islamic fundamentalists' success in controlling society is the depth and totality with which they suppress the freedom and rights of women. In Iran for 25 years, the ruling mullahs have enforced humiliating and sadistic rules and punishments on women and girls, enslaving them in a gender apartheid system of segregation, forced veiling, second-class status, lashing, and stoning to death.

Joining a global trend, the fundamentalists have added another way to dehumanize women and girls: buying and selling them for prostitution. Exact numbers of victims are impossible to obtain, but according to an official source in Tehran, there has been a 635 percent increase in the number of teenage girls

Donna M. Hughes, "Islamic Fundamentalism and the Sex Slave Trade in Iran," www.uri.edu/artsci/wms/hughes, January 27, 2004. Copyright © 2004 by Donna M. Hughes. Reproduced by permission.

in prostitution. The magnitude of this statistic conveys how rapidly this form of abuse has grown. In Tehran, there are an estimated 84,000 women and girls in prostitution, many of them are on the streets, others are in the 250 brothels that reportedly operate in the city. The trade is also international: thousands of Iranian women and girls have been sold into sexual slavery abroad.

Joining a global trend, the fundamentalists have added another way to dehumanize women and girls: buying and selling them for prostitution.

The head of Iran's Interpol bureau believes that the sex slave trade is one of the most profitable activities in Iran today. This criminal trade is not conducted outside the knowledge and participation of the ruling fundamentalists. Government officials themselves are involved in buying, selling, and sexually abusing women and girls.

Many of the girls come from impoverished rural areas. Drug addiction is epidemic throughout Iran, and some addicted parents sell their children to support their habits. High unemployment—28 percent for youth 15–29 years of age and 43 percent for women 15–20 years of age—is a serious factor in driving restless youth to accept risky offers for work. Slave traders take advantage of any opportunity in which women and children are vulnerable. For example, following the recent [2003] earthquake in Bam, orphaned girls have been kidnapped and taken to a known slave market in Tehran where Iranian and foreign traders meet.

Destination for the victims

Popular destinations for victims of the slave trade are the Arab countries in the Persian Gulf. According to the head of the Tehran province judiciary, traffickers target girls between 13 and 17, although there are reports of some girls as young as 8 and 10, to send to Arab countries. One ring was discovered after an 18-year-old girl escaped from a basement where a group of girls were held before being sent to Qatar, Kuwait and the United

Arab Emirates. The number of Iranian women and girls who are deported from Persian Gulf countries indicates the magnitude of the trade. Upon their return to Iran, the Islamic fundamentalists blame the victims, and often physically punish and imprison them. The women are examined to determine if they have engaged in "immoral activity." Based on the findings, officials can ban them from leaving the country again.

Police have uncovered a number of prostitution and slavery rings operating from Tehran that have sold girls to France, Britain, Turkey, as well. One network based in Turkey bought smuggled Iranian women and girls, gave them fake passports, and transported them to European and Persian Gulf countries. In one case, a 16-year-old girl was smuggled to Turkey, and then sold to a 58-year-old European national for $20,000.

In the northeastern Iranian province of Khorasan, local police report that girls are being sold to Pakistani men as sex slaves. The Pakistani men marry the girls, ranging in age from 12 to 20, and then sell them to brothels called "Kharabat" in Pakistan. One network was caught contacting poor families around Mashad and offering to marry girls. The girls were then taken through Afghanistan to Pakistan where they were sold to brothels.

Thousands of Iranian girls reportedly have been sold to Afghani men.

In the southeastern border province of Sistan Baluchestan, thousands of Iranian girls reportedly have been sold to Afghani men. Their final destinations are unknown.

One factor contributing to the increase in prostitution and the sex slave trade is the number of teen girls who are running away from home. The girls are rebelling against fundamentalist imposed restrictions on their freedom, domestic abuse, and parental drug addictions. Unfortunately, in their flight to freedom, the girls find more abuse and exploitation. Ninety percent of girls who run away from home will end up in prostitution. As a result of runaways, in Tehran alone there are an estimated 25,000 street children, most of them girls. Pimps prey upon street children, runaways, and vulnerable high school girls in city parks. In one case, a woman was discovered selling Iranian girls to men in Persian Gulf countries; for four years, she had hunted down runaway girls and sold them. She even sold her own daughter for US$11,000.

Authorities are involved in the exploitation

Given the totalitarian rule in Iran, most organized activities are known to the authorities. The exposure of sex slave networks in Iran has shown that many mullahs and officials are involved in the sexual exploitation and trade of women and girls. Women report that in order to have a judge approve a divorce they have to have sex with him. Women who are arrested for prostitution say they must have sex with the arresting officer. There are reports of police locating young women for sex for the wealthy and powerful mullahs.

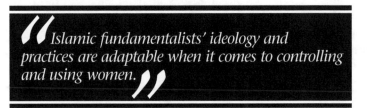

Islamic fundamentalists' ideology and practices are adaptable when it comes to controlling and using women.

In cities, shelters have been set up to provide assistance for runaways. Officials who run these shelters are often corrupt; they run prostitution rings using the girls from the shelter. For example in Karaj, the former head of a Revolutionary Tribunal and seven other senior officials were arrested in connection with a prostitution ring that used 12- to 18-year-old girls from a shelter called the Center of Islamic Orientation.

Other instances of corruption abound. There was a judge in Karaj who was involved in a network that identified young girls to be sold abroad. And in Qom, the center for religious training in Iran, when a prostitution ring was broken up, some of the people arrested were from government agencies, including the Department of Justice.

The views of ruling fundamentalists

The ruling fundamentalists have differing opinions on their official position on the sex trade: deny and hide it or recognize and accommodate it. In 2002, a BBC journalist was deported for taking photographs of prostitutes. Officials told her: "We are deporting you . . . because you have taken pictures of prostitutes. This is not a true reflection of life in our Islamic Republic. We don't have prostitutes." Yet, earlier the same year, officials of the Social Department of the Interior Ministry suggested legalizing prostitution as a way to manage it and control the spread of HIV. They proposed setting up brothels, called "morality houses," and using the traditional religious custom of temporary marriage, in which a couple can marry for a short period of time, even an hour, to facilitate prostitution. Islamic fundamentalists' ideology and practices are adaptable when it comes to controlling and using women.

Some may think a thriving sex trade in a theocracy with clerics acting as pimps is a contradiction in a country founded and ruled by Islamic fundamentalists. In fact, this is not a contradiction. First, exploitation and repression of women are closely associated. Both exist where women, individually or collectively, are denied freedom and rights. Second, the Islamic fundamentalists in Iran are not simply conservative Muslims. Islamic fundamentalism is a political movement with a political ideology that considers women inherently inferior in intellectual and moral capacity. Fundamentalists hate women's minds and bodies. Selling women and girls for prostitution is just the dehumanizing complement to forcing women and girls to cover their bodies and hair with the veil.

In a religious dictatorship like Iran, one cannot appeal to the rule of law for justice for women and girls. Women and girls have no guarantees of freedom and rights, and no expectation of respect or dignity from the Islamic fundamentalists. Only the end of the Iranian regime will free women and girls from all the forms of slavery they suffer.

12

Women Are Blamed for Being Raped in Islamic Countries

Robert Spencer

Robert Spencer is the director of Jihad Watch, a nonprofit organization that focuses on alerting the public about what it considers the dangers of radical Islam and the role of jihad in wars around the world. He has studied Islam for more than twenty years and is the author of Onward Muslim Soldiers: How Jihad Still Threatens America and the West *and* Islam Unveiled: Disturbing Questions About the World's Fastest Growing Faith. *He is coauthor, with Daniel Ali, of* Inside Islam: A Guide for Catholics.

A Frenchwoman who was raped by three men in the United Arab Emirates faces eighteen months in prison, while her attackers go free. By bringing the charge of rape, women under Islamic law incriminate themselves in the crime of unlawful sexual activity. Islamic women therefore generally hesitate to file rape charges for fear that they will be imprisoned, accused of having unlawful sexual relations, or raped again by police officials. The punishment for sex outside of marriage ranges from imprisonment to death. The international community must continue to pressure Islamic countries to reform their unjust laws.

"For almost a year," observes Edward Said in this week's [January 23, 2003] edition of Cairo's *Al-Ahram Weekly*, "American politicians, regional experts, administration officials, journalists have repeated the charges that have become standard fare so far as Islam and the Arabs are concerned. . . . To today's practically unanimous chorus has been added the authority of the United Nations' Human Development Report on the Arab world which certified that Arabs dramatically lag behind the rest of the world in democracy, knowledge, and women's rights."

Said has no more patience for this sort of thing than he did when he wrote *Orientalism* and *Covering Islam*, the twin towers of today's academic Islamophilia. He acidly dismisses the criticisms as "vague re-cycled Orientalist clichés."

Yet just as Said's lament appeared, the French businesswoman Touria Tiouli went to court in the United Arab Emirates.[1] Heedlessly risking the recycling of vague Orientalist clichés, Dubai officials have turned her charge that she was raped by three men on its head and accused her of *zina*, sexual activity outside marriage. In Dubai, a bastion of moderate Islam, this charge isn't punishable by stoning, as it is in more hard-line Muslim countries—it only carries an 18-month jail sentence.

Tiouli continues to fight: on Sunday she entered a not guilty plea. To the claims of her attackers that she was a willing participant and, in fact, a prostitute whom they duly paid, she replied simply, "My lawyer will prove I did not consent. If I had consented, I would not have brought the case."

These cases all unfolded according to the classic directives of the Sharia.

Indeed, it's hard to imagine a prostitute in Dubai going to the police willingly under any circumstances. For Sharia courts all over the Islamic world seem only too willing to reinforce the stereotypes of Islam that Said deplores, particularly where women are concerned. In Nigeria, a woman named Sufiyatu

1. Touria Tiouli was born in Casablanca on October 15, 1963. She has lived in France since her early childhood and is a French citizen. On October 14, 2002, during a visit to Dubai, United Arab Emirates (UAE), she was raped by three men. She identified her attackers, who accused her of being a prostitute. Touria was charged and prevented from leaving the country for six months while the judicial process continued. With the intervention of the French Embassy, her passport was returned to her and she was allowed to leave Dubai for her home in France. Her status under UAE law is unclear, and she could be the subject of further criminal actions by the UAE government. Her attackers have never been charged.

Huseini suffered through circumstances remarkably similar to Tiouli's. She said she was raped, but the man she accused denied it, and instead Huseini was charged with adultery.

Nigeria is no moderate Dubai: Huseini faced death by stoning until the verdict was overturned under international pressure. Countless other women in similar situations have already been stoned to death or jailed. According to Sisters in Islam, a Malaysian advocacy group for Muslim women, in Pakistan "three out of four women in prison . . . are rape victims."

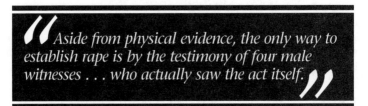

Aside from physical evidence, the only way to establish rape is by the testimony of four male witnesses . . . who actually saw the act itself.

This blame-the-victim mentality should be the worst nightmare of American feminists, were it not for the fact that they view it through rosy multiculturalist glasses. But does it really represent the hijacking of the Religion of Peace on a grand scale?

Not quite. These cases all unfolded according to the classic directives of the Sharia.

Traditional Islamic law, which is still very much in force in Saudi Arabia, Pakistan, Iran, Sudan, most (if not all) of post-Taliban Afghanistan, and elsewhere, completely disregards the testimony of women in cases of a sexual nature. Aside from physical evidence, the only way to establish rape is by the testimony of four male witnesses (who, by the way, must be Muslims in good standing) who actually saw the act itself. Without these witnesses and a confession from the accused rapist, the victim will stand condemned by her very accusation: she wasn't raped, so she must be guilty of *zina*.

Moreover, the prosecution has been careful to point out that Tiouli didn't call for help. "According to Islamic Sharia," says the Nigerian Imam Mallam Muhammad Sani Isa, "it cannot be considered rape unless you asked for help."

According to Aliyu Abubakar Sanyinna, the attorney general of Nigeria's Zamfara state (where Huseini went through her ordeal), this codified miscarriage of justice is "the law of Allah. By executing anybody that is convicted under Islamic law, we are just complying with the laws of Allah, so we don't have anything to worry about."

If like minds prevail, . . . in Dubai when the court issues a verdict in Tiouli's case, she should resign herself to spending the next eighteen months behind bars.

There is yet hope. International indignation resulted in the overturning of Huseini's death sentence and the commutation of a similar ruling against an 18-year-old Christian girl in Sudan, Abok Alfa Akok, to 75 lashes. Facing another worldwide outcry, the Nigerian government promised in October [2002] to end stonings for adultery. Also bowing to internal and external pressure, even the Islamic Republic of Iran declared early this year [2003] that it too was ending the practice.

All this is good, but it isn't enough. Rape victims in these newly enlightened nations may not have to fear stoning but they still may face lighter sentences, as does Tiouli. They will continue to receive no sympathy for their ordeal or any honest investigation of the charges they have made.

Until the Sharia itself undergoes a thoroughgoing reevaluation, this is probably the best we can hope for. Thus—however much Edward Said and his ilk may gnash their teeth—those who traffic in "vague re-cycled Orientalist clichés" about women's rights in the Islamic world must keep up the pressure.

13

Iraq's Clerics Are Imposing Strict Dress Codes on Women

Ilene R. Prusher

Ilene R. Prusher is a staff writer for the Christian Science Monitor, *an international newspaper.*

The Hawza clerics in Iraq are refusing to allow women who are not dressed in extremely conservative clothing to enter mosques for worship. Although the women are dressed in the Islamic head scarf and wear a long gown called the *jupeh,* the clerics consider their clothing immodest. Although the clerics say they have not created new dress codes for women, the armed guards at the mosques are not allowing entrance to women without head-to-toe cloaks.

The only parts of Maryam Mohammed and Zeinab Sarowa visible to the world are their hands and faces. But when they come for Friday prayers at the Shiite mosque where they have worshiped all their lives, they are turned away.

The reason: though covered head to toe, they're not wearing the dark, billowing clothing the guard says is required for Muslim women during prayer.

Sulking with her friends outside one of Baghdad's holiest Shiite shrines in the neighborhood of Kadhumiya, Ms. Mohammed says that in the past, even when visiting the world-famous Shiite sites in Najaf and Karbala, no one questioned her dress or barred her from entering.

But that was then. In the new Iraq, religious groups, once under the stifling control of Saddam Hussein, are testing out their newfound elbow room. Some Iraqis view this as the unfettering of faith after decades of a Baathist regime that brutally suppressed religion, particularly the majority Shiites. For others, many women in particular, it is as if the piercing summer sun, which bathes the courtyard of the shrine, is also drying up their liberties before their eyes.

"Thursday they sent my sister away. Who are they? Who put them in charge?" snaps Ms. Sarowa, who finished a political science degree [in 2001], but has yet to find a job. "If there were a government here, they wouldn't be able to do that."

There is an authority of sorts at the shrine containing the tomb of Imam Musa al-Kadhum and his grandson, for whom the neighborhood is named. It is called the Hawza el Miya, which is the world's foremost seminary of Shiite religious learning. It is made up of 1,000 scholars who are authorized to issue *fatwas*, or religious edicts. The word of the Hawza is considered the most authoritative in the Shiite world, and presents a challenge even to the clerics in Iran's holy city of Qom, whose role was elevated by the flight of Iraqi religious leaders during Mr. Hussein's rule.

It is the Hawza, says an armed guard actively turning away women who are not in *abaya*, who has ordered the enforcement of this new dress code.

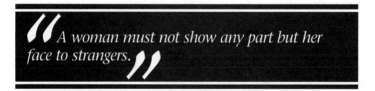

A woman must not show any part but her face to strangers.

Both Mohammed and Sarowa are wearing long, light-colored suit-jackets, floor-length skirts, and *hijab*, or an Islamic head scarf. But they are not, the guard at door of the dazzling mosque and Shiite shrine complains, wearing the *abaya*. The *abaya*, a big and billowing head-to-toe black cloth that is placed over a long black cloak—which itself is worn over a woman's indoor clothing—with a separate, tightly fastened head scarf, is similar to the *chador* worn by many women in Iran. What Iraqis call the *jupeh*, a long, straight-cut gown similar to the Western equivalent of a housedress, is not sufficient, says Said Alla Azaidi.

"My dear sister," he tells an inquiring woman, "it is an order from the Hawza of Najaf, because all of the body of a woman should be protected. A woman must not show any part but her face to strangers." The coat she wears "must be wide," he says, at least when she's coming to a religious establishment.

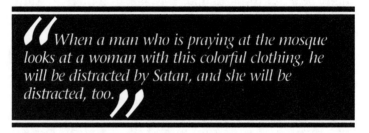

When a man who is praying at the mosque looks at a woman with this colorful clothing, he will be distracted by Satan, and she will be distracted, too.

The policy, Mr. Azaidi says, began to be instituted after the fall of Mr. Hussein's regime.

"The [long dresses] which open in the front with buttons, that's no good. We don't consider that lawful *hijab*," Azaidi continues. Nor are light or pastel fabrics, like the whites and blues worn by Mohammed and Sarowa approved.

"When a man who is praying at the mosque looks at a woman with this colorful clothing, he will be distracted by Satan, and she will be distracted, too," he says. The policy could not be enforced in the past, he adds, because "Saddam Hussein was persecuting the Shiites and he didn't want a Muslim society."

No jeans for "real" Muslims

The quickly evolving dress code is not limited to mosques. At Al Mustansirriye University in Baghdad, new guidelines have been posted on student bulletin boards by "security officers" who say they have been elected to represent the Hawza on campus. One professor complains that Baath Party enforcers are just being replaced by Hawza authorities.

Signs near the campus entrance state: "A [new version of the] *hijab* appeared in Iraq after the year 2000 in which girls leave part of the head uncovered. Although this is called the French *hijab*, it is made in Iraq and is widespread in institutions and universities. Therefore we address all believers. They should ask representatives of the Hawza for their opinions about such *hijab* and whether it is allowed."

The sign then goes on to provide an answer from Ayatollah

Sheikh Mohammed El Yacuby, an expert on social problems. "The woman who wears such *hijab* is not a real Muslim and she has no belief in Islam. There is no permission for this kind of *hijab*," the Ayatollah's response reads. The sign goes on to state that pants, jeans, or culottes are also not allowed.

With such notices popping up in various places, several women complain that they fear things are getting worse, not better, as a result of the US-led invasion. The coalition authorities occupying Iraq have pledged that they will do everything possible to ensure that the new Iraq will empower all groups, including women. L. Paul Bremer, the US civilian administrator in Iraq, says the political council of 25 to 30 members he is appointing next month will certainly include women.

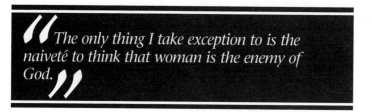

The only thing I take exception to is the naiveté to think that woman is the enemy of God.

It is not just women who are concerned about religious Shiite muscle flexing.

"The only thing I take exception to is the naiveté to think that woman is the enemy of God. They are imposing *hijab*, but only in certain [areas]," says Dr. Wamidh Nadhmi, a professor of political science at Baghdad University. "I wouldn't be reluctant to write articles saying, 'You are making fools of yourselves in imposing the *hijab*, and not just *hijab*, but *abaya*.'"

No imitating Americans

The sudden strictness appears to be applied by zealous individuals who have appointed themselves to the task, and may not be an actual modesty police with authority to enforce new rules.

"We don't have a new policy toward women these days," says Mullah Hamid Rashid al Saadi, a cleric from Sadr City, a poor and predominantly Shiite area that was once forced to call itself Saddam City. "The commitment to wear these things comes from the heart. You cannot enforce it."

That hasn't stopped the guardians at the gates of Kadhumiya. Different guards were spotted turning away women not wearing *abaya*. In one case, a woman wearing a long black robe and a golden-yellow head scarf—but not the *abaya*—was told to stay out. When a foreign reporter approached her to ask her what happened, the guard said: "I'll let you in this time, but don't come back like this again." The woman, who declined to give her name, was insulted. "I do not consider myself Sunni or Shiite," she says, "I am just a Muslim, and I have always come here."

Some women say the guards are being reasonable. Women should wear the *abaya* to attend prayers, some say, and should not come dressed stylishly in pants "like the Sunni women used to be able to," one woman said, as her friends agreed.

Mothers with adolescent girls not in *abaya* were told that they could come in if they walked with their daughters covered inside the wing of the mother's *abayas*.

When Friday prayers come at about one o'clock in the afternoon, worshipers listen to a sermon by Sayed Hazem al-Aragy, a cleric who has just returned from exile in Iran.

"The Iraqi people should keep away from the American forces. Students in universities have a heavy task for themselves: to try to stop anyone who tries to imitate the American style, either in dress or in thought," Mr. Aragy said, "because they are trying to spoil Islam and the Muslim shrines."

The young women, disappointed that they could not attend prayers, decided to go shopping instead. "Why are they doing this now? It is important to put freedom in place first. I am ready to go to complain to a human rights organization," says Sarowa. Realistically, she did not expect anyone, especially not the US soldiers sparsely patrolling this neighborhood, to get involved. "Who can say anything to the Hawza? This is a problem for us."

14

Muslim Dress Does Not Oppress Islamic Women

Laila Al-Marayati and Semeen Issa

Laila Al-Marayati, a Los Angeles physician, and Semeen Issa, a schoolteacher in Arcadia, California, are the spokesperson and president, respectively, for the Muslim Women's League.

Many Westerners assume that Muslim women wearing traditional veils or *hijab* are either oppressed or are fundamentalist zealots. These assumptions are simplistic. Muslim women are diverse and have various reasons for wearing *hijab*. Although some Muslim governments have used dress codes to yield power over women, it is not the clothing that is oppressive but despotic regimes that subjugate Muslim men and women alike. Islamic women who dress modestly by choice should not be accused of caving in to male domination. A woman's worth should rest in her accomplishments, not her clothing.

A few years ago, someone from the Feminist Majority Foundation called the Muslim Women's League to ask if she could "borrow a burka"[1] for a photo shoot the organization was doing to draw attention to the plight of women in Afghanistan under the Taliban. When we told her that we didn't have one, and that none of our Afghan friends did either, she expressed surprise, as if she'd assumed that all Muslim women keep burkas in their closets in case a militant Islamist comes to dinner. She didn't seem to understand that her assumption was the equiva-

---

1. a garment that covers the entire face, head and body

lent of assuming that every Latino has a Mexican sombrero in their closet.

We don't mean to make light of the suffering of our sisters in Afghanistan, but the burka was—and is—not their major focus of concern. Their priorities are more basic, like feeding their children, becoming literate and living free from violence. Nevertheless, recent articles in the Western media suggest the burka means everything to Muslim women, because they routinely express bewilderment at the fact that all Afghan women didn't cast off their burkas when the Taliban was defeated. The Western press' obsession with the dress of Muslim women is not surprising, however, since the press tends to view Muslims, in general, simplistically.

Misunderstandings in the Western media

Headlines in the mainstream media have reduced Muslim female identity to an article of clothing—"the veil." One is hard-pressed to find an article, book or film about women in Islam that doesn't have "veil" in the title: "Behind the Veil," "Beyond the Veil," "At the Drop of a Veil" and more. The use of the term borders on the absurd: Perhaps next will come "What Color is Your Veil?" or "Rebel Without a Veil" or "Whose Veil is it, Anyway?"

The word "veil" does not even have a universal meaning. In some cultures, it refers to a face-covering known as niqab; in others, to a simple head scarf, known as hijab. Other manifestations of "the veil" include all-encompassing outer garments like the ankle-length abaya from the Persian Gulf states, the chador in Iran or the burka in Afghanistan.

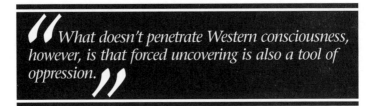

What doesn't penetrate Western consciousness, however, is that forced uncovering is also a tool of oppression.

Like the differences in our clothing from one region to another, Muslim women are diverse. Stereotypical assumptions about Muslim women are as inaccurate as the assumption that all American women are personified by the bikini-clad cast of "Baywatch." Anyone who has spent time interacting with Muslims knows that, despite numerous obstacles, Muslim women are active, assertive and engaged in society. In Qatar, women make up the majority of graduate-school students. The Iranian parliament has more women members than the U.S. Senate. Throughout the world, many Muslim women are educated and professionally trained; they participate in public debates, are often catalysts for reform and champions for their own rights. At the same time, there is no denying that in many Muslim countries, dress has been used as a tool to wield power over women.

Uncovering by force

What doesn't penetrate Western consciousness, however, is that forced uncovering is also a tool of oppression. During the reign of Shah Mohammad Reza Pahlavi in Iran, wearing the veil was prohibited. As an expression of their opposition to his repressive regime, women who supported the 1979 Islamic Revolution marched in the street clothed in chadors. Many of them did not expect to have this "dress code" institutionalized by those who led the revolution and then took power in the new government.

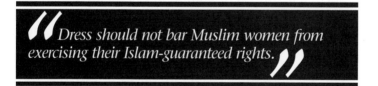

Dress should not bar Muslim women from exercising their Islam-guaranteed rights.

In Turkey, the secular regime considers the head scarf a symbol of extremist elements that want to overthrow the government. Accordingly, women who wear any type of head-covering are banned from public office, government jobs and academia, including graduate school. Turkish women who believe the head-covering is a religious obligation are unfairly forced to give up public life or opportunities for higher education and career advancement.

Dress should not bar Muslim women from exercising their Islam-guaranteed rights, like the right to be educated, to earn a living and to move about safely in society. Unfortunately, some governments impose a strict dress code along with other restrictions, like limiting education for women, to appear "authentically Islamic." Such laws, in fact, are inconsistent with Islam. Nevertheless, these associations lead to the general perception that "behind the veil" lurk other, more insidious examples of the repression of women, and that wearing the veil somehow causes the social ills that plague Muslim women around the world.

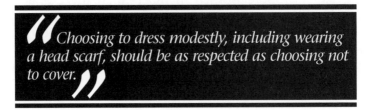

Choosing to dress modestly, including wearing a head scarf, should be as respected as choosing not to cover.

Many Muslim men and women alike are subjugated by despotic, dictatorial regimes. Their lot in life is worsened by extreme poverty and illiteracy, two conditions that are not caused by Islam but are sometimes exploited in the name of religion. Helping Muslim women overcome their misery is a major task. The reconstruction of Muslim Afghanistan will be a test case for the Afghan people and for the international community dedicated to making Afghan society work for everyone. To some, Islam is the root cause of the problems faced by women in Afghanistan. But what is truly at fault is a misguided, narrow interpretation of Islam designed to serve a rigid patriarchal system.

Traditional Muslim populations will be more receptive to change that is based on Islamic principles of justice, as expressed in the Koran, than they will be to change that abandons religion altogether or confines it to private life. Muslim scholars and leaders who emphasize Islamic principles that support women's rights to education, health care, marriage and divorce, equal pay for equal work and participation in public life could fill the vacuum now occupied by those who impose a vision of Islam that infringes on the rights of women.

Dress is irrelevant

Given the opportunity, Muslim women, like women everywhere, will become educated, pursue careers, strive to do what is best for their families and contribute positively according to their abilities. How they dress is irrelevant. It should be obvious that the critical element Muslim women need is freedom, especially the freedom to make choices that enable them to be independent agents of positive change. Choosing to dress modestly, including wearing a head scarf, should be as respected as choosing not to cover. Accusations that modestly dressed Muslim women are caving in to male-dominated understandings of Islam neglect the reality that most Muslim women who cover by choice do so out of subservience to God, not to any human being.

The worth of a woman—any woman—should not be determined by the length of her skirt, but by the dedication, knowledge and skills she brings to the task at hand.

15

The Debate over the Head-Scarf Ban in Turkey Is Still Heated

Serpil Karacan Sellars

Serpil Karacan Sellars is a freelance journalist based in Istanbul, Turkey.

Turkey, a secular state with a large Muslim population, banned the Islamic head scarf in many areas of public life in the 1980s. Since then, many Muslim women who choose to wear the head scarf have faced discrimination in schools, courts, and hospitals. Some believe that the ban is a violation of their rights to express their religious devotion. On the other hand, many Turkish women support the head scarf ban because they view the garb as a dangerous symbol of oppressive regimes such as those of Iran or Algeria, where women are forced to cover their heads.

The overwhelming vote by France's lower house of parliament in February [2004] to ban religious symbols in state schools—mainly directed at the Islamic headscarf—certainly resonates in Turkey.

For more than two decades a battle over headscarves has raged in staunchly secular but Muslim-majority Turkey, where women are forbidden to wear the Islamic headscarf in public places, most notably state schools and government institutions.

The ban affects thousands of female students forced to boycott schools and universities. Teachers who refuse to enforce the ban have been fired and charged under anti-terrorist laws.

In late 2003, the ban dominated media headlines when President Ahmet Necdet Sezar refused to invite veiled wives of members of the ruling party to a palace reception.

Nevertheless, secular groups such as Turkey's military, many academics, feminists and writers welcome the French decision.

"In Turkey, the turban [as the traditional Islamic headscarf is known] has always been an issue of 'backwardness' against 'modernity'," says Ayse Kadioglu, a professor at the Political Science Department at the Sabanci University.

For secularists, the French decision provided a sound Western justification for the Turkish ban, even though a recent study shows 64% of Turkish women wear the headscarf.

Fundamentalists and the headscarf

The French government believes the ban will not only protect its secular traditions, but help repel rising Islamic fundamentalism—a fear dominating much of the West, post September 11.

Ironically in Muslim Turkey, fear of Islamic fundamentalism also lies behind official hostility to the headscarf. The military's opposition is particularly fierce, a legacy of its 1923 mandate from the founder of the Turkish Republic, the reformer Kemel Ataturk, to protect the new, secular state.

Although women wear headscarves for a myriad of reasons, including religious devotion, modesty and as a sign of political affiliation, the garment has come to symbolise a wider battle over what sort of state Turkey should be.

Many commentators believe that in order to justify its immense power the army needs external threats—such as Kurdish nationalism, left-wing activity and political Islam—to maintain its position.

Women wearing headscarves have been refused treatment at state medical facilities.

General Hursit Tolon, commander of Turkey's Aegean Army, calls the headscarf ban an "antidote [to] fundamentalism".

Kenan Evren, Turkey's president from 1982 to 1989 and chief of staff during the 1980 military coup, claims that the rise of political Islam in Turkey —which includes the growing number of women wearing the turban—is linked to countries such as Iran which seek to export shariah, or Islamic law, to Turkey. "There were a handful of them [in 1980]," he said of women wearing headscarves. "But today there are thousands, tens of thousands . . . you have to crush the sleeping snake before it bites you." Evren's war-like metaphor is no accident. When the ruling Muslim Justice and Development Party (AKP) introduced a draft law after its 2002 election victory to extend the areas women could wear the headscarf, the opposition Republican People's Party (CHP) founded by Ataturk publicly warned that extending the boundaries where women can wear the headscarf would take place "only through a bloody Islamic revolution". The headscarf is banned in public buildings and state schools, and in recent years enforcement of the ban has been tightened to include religious schools. According to human rights activist and lawyer Eren Keskin, political parties have been shut down by the courts for promoting its greater acceptance. Women wearing headscarves have been refused treatment at state medical facilities, and in November 2003 a veiled defendant was ordered from a courtroom by the presiding judge, who said she "had no right to be in a public area—a courthouse".

Many Turkish women support the headscarf ban.

According to Professor Ali Yasar Saribay of Uludag University's Political Sociology Department, the judge's ruling sat a dangerous precedent—the issue could one day arise of whether to allow veiled women on public transport.

However, one state prosecutor, who requested anonymity, defended the ruling, arguing: "The turban is used as an uprising against the main principle of secularism and leads to religion-based hatred . . . and endangers public order."

Others believe that enforcing and extending the ban is opportunistic—when pro-Islamic parties like the ruling AKP win elections—and profoundly unfair toward ordinary women, like Aysegul Yilmaz, a student at Marmara University. Unlike moderate Islamist Prime Minster Recap Erdogan's daughters—who have the financial means to study abroad in the United States where they wear headscarves on campus—Yilmaz has to go bareheaded in order to attend classes.

"We had high hopes of this government but they have not moved an inch on the issue of the headscarf ban. In fact it has worsened since they came to power, and worst of all Europe has never listened to our voice," says Gulden Sonmez of Mazlumder, an Islamist human rights group.

Ibrahim Yildirim, AKP branch deputy chairman of the conservative Fatih district in Istanbul, concedes the charge: "There are issues where our hands are tied," he says. "And yet there are more severe problems in the society, such as economic hardship, to deal with."

Many Turkish women support the headscarf ban. "I find that it can be very dangerous personally," says Ayse Oncu, a sociology professor at Sabanci University. "I fear the kinds of regimes that resemble those of Saudi Arabia, Iran, even Egypt."

Ayse Bohurler, Turkey's only headscarf-wearing television presenter and an AKP founding member, dismisses the possibility. "I do not see an Afghanistan . . . in Turkey, since the dynamics and culture of the society are very different," she says, noting the tolerance of the old Ottoman Empire to its minorities, including Spain's exiled Sephardic Jews.

Rights activist Sanar Yurdatapan is not convinced. "We don't want to be an Algeria or an Iran, a country where women are forced to wear head coverings," she told *The Chicago Tribune.* "But what is the difference between forcing someone to wear something or requiring them to take it off? The human rights are the same."

More fundamentally, Prof. Oncu says, the question of the headscarf is one of inequalities between men and women. "It is the women's dress code that is again being debated by the male world."

16

American Muslim Women Need to Develop an Egalitarian Islam

Gwendolyn Zoharah Simmons

Gwendolyn Zoharah Simmons is an assistant professor of religion at the University of Florida. She is a Sufi Muslim who studied for more than seventeen years with the Sufi mystic Sheikh Muhammad Raheem Bawa Muhaiyadeen. Her areas of expertise include Islamic progressive reform and the impact of Islamic law on Muslim women.

Women are generally oppressed in Islamic societies as men define women's roles and severely limit their opportunities. Yet the basis of discrimination is not to be found in the Koran, which contains many verses that support equality for women. Since the eighth century, however, Islamic authorities have propagated misogynist interpretations to justify violence and repression against women. Muslims and feminists in the United States must fight to reinterpret the Koranic texts and practice an Islam that is egalitarian in its precepts.

Any attempt to write about "women and human rights" in an Islamic context for me is extremely difficult. It is difficult because of all of my experiences with the Islamic tradition . . . both in the Middle East and here in the U.S.A. No matter

Gwendolyn Zoharah Simmons, "Are We Up to the Challenge? The Need for a Radical Re-Ordering of the Islamic Discourse on Women," *Progressive Muslims: On Justice, Gender, and Pluralism,* edited by Omid Safi. Oxford, UK: Oneworld Publications, 2003, pp. 233–48. Copyright © 2003 by Oneworld Publications. Reproduced by permission.

the level of rationalizations (apologetic or explanatory), what I have seen and heard regarding the status of women in Islam has been, for the most part, discriminatory to women. Frankly, I am tired of the contortions, the bending over backwards, and the justifications for the oppressive, repressive, and exclusionary treatment of women in majority Islamic societies as well as in minority Muslim communities in the U.S.A. I for one cannot and do not accept the justifications or rationalizations for this current reality. To me, these practices are morally wrong. Just as slavery cannot be morally justified today, neither can the contemporary suppression of or discrimination against women be justified. . . .

I personally became engaged in a vigorous fight for my self, for my identity as a black person who had grown up in a racist society at an early age. I was greatly aided in my struggle for self and agency by the black women in my home (my mother, my grandmother, my aunts), my church (particularly the women leaders of the church), my school (wonderful women teachers who took me under their wings and nurtured my intellect and my spirit), and in my community (women community leaders who encouraged my talents and my leadership abilities). I am fortunate as an African-American woman to have been surrounded by powerful women role models who had survived incredible hardships to make a way out of no way.

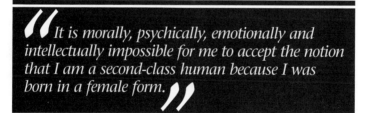

It is morally, psychically, emotionally and intellectually impossible for me to accept the notion that I am a second-class human because I was born in a female form.

I was further aided in my struggle against racial dehumanization by the African-American interpretation of Christianity, which not only imputed agency to African-Americans, male and female, but also a chosenness and a challenge to rise up from the degradation and humiliations imposed by our enemies to become a model community of faith and righteousness. I was blessed to be nurtured in such a religious environment.

I came into Islam with this history, with this legacy. Therefore, it is morally, psychically, emotionally and intellectually impossible for me to accept the notion that I am a second-class human because I was born in a female form. I can no more accept this idea than I could accept in the 1960s that I was a second-class citizen because I was born in a black body. My feminism has been greatly informed by my experiences gleaned in the fight for equality here in racist America.

An Islam that teaches equality

I am further strengthened in my beliefs about the equality of women by the fact that I was graced by God to meet a Sufi[1] mystic, Sheikh Muhammad Raheem Bawa Muhaiyaddeen, who by his teachings, his example, and his very being introduced me to Islam, an Islam of justice, truth, beauty, and grace. The Islam that my Sheikh taught and exemplified is a gender, racial, and religiously egalitarian Islam. It is an Islam that teaches that all human beings are created from a divine ray of God, are all God's children and are completely equal in God's sight. It is an Islam that overtly acknowledges the feminine qualities of God, those qualities of wisdom, compassion, nurturance, and sustenance. It is an Islam that teaches that the human being has been endowed with seven levels of consciousness or wisdom through which he or she can know God personally. The way to know God personally, intimately, taught Bawa Muhaiyaddeen, is through a rigorous self-purification process whereby all ideas and feelings of separation (sexual, racial, and religious), and the ego sense are purged. To be a Muslim, taught Bawa Muhaiyaddeen, is to be in a state of purity. If one reaches this "state" of Islam, this state of purity, then one can communicate directly with God, taught Bawa. Then one is truly a *Mu'min* (a pure believer). It is then and only then that one can truly understand the Qur'an, one's duty to God and one's fellow beings, human, animal, and plant, taught Bawa. This was the Islam that captured my heart.

In my studies of Islam, I see Bawa's teachings and that of many others in the Sufi and philosophical streams in Islam as the true essence of Islam, which emerges after one strips away the cultural, racial, and ideological accretions and dross. It is then and only then, says Bawa, that the human being steps into the true radiance and beauty of God Consciousness, which recognizes no differences in the human family. In this state, all are seen as potential manifestations of God, made in the image of God, which in the physical takes two forms, male and female.

1. a branch of Islamic philosophy that believes in the immediate consciousness of the transcendent nature of God

It is only this physical form that has differences and these are for reproductive purposes. The soul, the *qalb* (heart), and the levels of consciousness are not differentiated according to race or gender but are potentially the same. To see differences and to make distinctions based on differences in color, class, or gender is the greatest ignorance, taught Bawa Muhaiyaddeen.

Theory vs. practice of Islam

However, what I have found in Islam, as practiced, is very, very different from Bawa's teachings. Distinctions based on race, skin color, class, gender, and religion occur all the time in societies and communities that call themselves Muslim. From my Bawa Muhaiyaddeen inspired vantage, it seems that one of the primordial essences of the religion of Islam is justice. The Islam that I embrace in my heart is one of peace and justice. There can be no peace where there is unrelenting injustice. The injustice to which Muslim women have been subjected cannot be said to be the will of a God of justice. When the oppression of women occurs in an Islamic society in the name of Islam, it is the result of many things, religious, cultural, and economic. Certainly one of these is men's incorrect interpretations of the Qur'an and *hadith* owing to the societal and cultural influences that shaped the early jurists' and theologians' worldview and subsequent interpretation of these texts. It is not because Islam requires it any more than any of the other religions require it. These early anti-women interpretations have been compounded by later misogynist accretions to Islam's canon and the mistaken belief that what the earlier doctors of law and theology decided are immutable, unchangeable. This has locked us as Muslims into a legal and theological prison that has fostered and justified violence and repression against women and religious minorities which are done in the name of God and religion. . . .

Male authorities oppress women

Men defined and continue to define what is in the best interest of Muslim societies legally. Many of the male authorities did not then and do not now include the best interests of over half of their population, women and girls, in their legal formulations. Laws, for example, that continue to countenance universal and unrestricted divorce privileges for men while placing severe restrictions on women's ability to obtain a divorce; those that permit unregulated polygamy; those that place restrictions on women's rights to travel, their right to decide if they will go to school or go to work outside the home if married; and those that give reduced sentences to male relatives who commit honor killings and the like are not taking women's interest seriously and are oblivious to the harms that such restrictions can and do cause women. These laws continue to buttress and sustain male privilege, patriarchal privilege, and to enforce women's subjugation and oppression.

> *It is an Islam that overtly acknowledges the feminine qualities of God, those qualities of wisdom, compassion, nurturance, and sustenance.*

Islam as practiced does have a gender ideology, which is not necessarily reflective of the Qur'an, which, as both Leila Ahmed and Farid Esack have written, shows ambivalence about women's equality. There is, however, a significant number of verses enjoining equitable treatment for women. So much so that if the male lawmakers had been so inclined, they could have developed a gender-equitable interpretation of the Qur'an. The negative position of women in Islamic societies has been deeply affected by the writings, interpretations, and attitudes of the *'ulama* of the eighth, ninth, and tenth centuries. Their attitudes regarding breadwinning in the family, Islamic family law, biological differences between the sexes, differences in the socialization of the sexes, and the whole issue of men's honor being located between the thighs of a woman have been used to marginalize women in both the public and domestic spheres. Polygamy, men's easy access to divorce, and the wife's expected obedience to her husband in all matters including sexual access and when to have or not have children, have marginalized women in the private sphere. Putting men in charge of household expenditures . . . is largely responsible for the socioeconomic inequality between the genders.

By and large, Muslim religious authorities and legal scholars are of the view that the man is obliged to provide food, shelter, and clothing for his wife and children. In return the woman has obligations toward her husband including obeying his sexual demands. According to male interpretations of Islam that have become the orthodox view, men because of their economic role are given the authority to manage the affairs of women and even to punish women if they do not obey. It should be admitted that men's absolute control over women seriously erodes those rights given to women in Islam that Muslims are so quick to brag about—the right to own and hold property, to work outside the home and to have control over their income, etc. If a man controls your movements and demands that you stay inside the house, it is pretty difficult for you to earn an income or to manage your properties.

Restrictions on women questioned

This whole idea that women have to be protected, looked after, and controlled must be re-examined. Also the prevalent notion that the morality of society can be upheld only through restrictions and policing of women must be challenged. Why the double standard on morality and chastity in Islamic societies and communities? The Qur'an commands chastity and sexual purity for both men and women. Certainly, we all want strong families with children who are cared for and protected by their mothers and their fathers. But if the creation and maintenance of such families become the rationale and justification for denying women human rights, then alternatives to keeping families strong and intact must be found. Resilient and together families can no longer rest on women and their behavior alone; men must assume their role as parents beyond the breadwinning function. We must challenge the idea that woman's destiny is biologically determined. The idea that women's biological differences produce an intellectual difference and an emotional difference that suits her for motherhood and home-making exclusively must be challenged and eradicated.

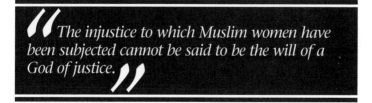

The injustice to which Muslim women have been subjected cannot be said to be the will of a God of justice.

In 2002, I went to hear a noted African-American imam speak at a major university as a guest of a Muslim student group.

I purchased three of his tapes that were being sold at that gathering. One of them was titled "The Nature of the Woman." I became very sad listening to the contents of that tape, which posits that women are created from a bent rib and as such have certain negative characteristics, which are an inherent part of her nature. The upshot of his discourse was that women were created to have a highly emotional nature, since this suits them for their role as bearers and caretakers of children. Implicit in his statements was the idea that this was woman's primary role. Here is an African-American man who seemingly has forgotten his own history and the legacy of his foremothers. He has forgotten, for example, that Harriet Tubman single-handedly escaped slavery in 1849 when she was twenty-nine years old, only to return nineteen times to lead three hundred other enslaved Africans to freedom. It is said that Tubman carried a gun in her waistband and if one of her passengers became terrified on the perilous journey and wanted to turn back, Tubman would threaten to kill him or her on the spot and forced them onward, onward to freedom. Tubman had a U.S. $40,000 bounty on her head and that was a lot of money in the 1850s. Traveling by night, hiding by day, scaling the mountains, fording the rivers, threading the forests, lying concealed as the pursuers passed them, Tubman led her passengers, guided by the North Star, to freedom. To this day, none knows the paths she took. But some say it must have been God who led her and I agree. Now can you tell me that this woman was too emotional to be a leader? She was not only a leader; she was a general. Tubman was the first woman soldier in the U.S. Army. She served as a scout and a guide during the Civil War. Shamefully, Tubman was a war veteran who had to sue the U.S. government to get her pension. I am going on at some length about my foremother Tubman as an antidote to this imam's tape that says that because woman is created from a rib she is emotional, and that her nature suits her exclusively for motherhood and wifely duties. Clearly women are created to be mothers, since it is only women who can give birth to children. Unfortunately, what is a wonderful attribute given by God to women has been turned into the justification for women's suppression, repression, and oppression. . . .

Universal issues for women

Feminist discourse among Muslim women in the Arab world has addressed universal issues including:

- the unfettered right to education and work outside the home;
- women's rights in marriage, divorce, and custody of children cases after divorce;
- women's right to the vote, to stand for election, and to participate in all spheres of their society;
- the right to travel freely and an end to gender segregation.

There is a long and wonderful history of Arab Muslim and Christian feminists as well as Muslim feminists in other parts of the Islamic world, including most notably those in Indonesia, Iran, Pakistan, and Turkey, who are striving for their full human rights. I am sure that many if not most Muslims in the world are unaware of this history. It is an important part of recent Islamic history that needs to be taught to Muslims the world over. I urge all Muslim women and progressive men to teach this history of Islamic feminism to Muslims everywhere. I hope that we feminist and progressive Muslims here in America will teach this history to all the women and men converts coming into Islam as well as the immigrants (male and female) who have come to America to live. Just as African-Americans have had to wrest our true history from the lies and obfuscations of white racist American history, we feminist and progressive Muslims must learn and teach the history of Muslim women's struggle for justice against ignorance, tradition, and superstition to all Muslims, especially the young. We will face formidable opposition in our efforts. Most likely we will be driven from our mosques and community centers when we try to teach this history. We will be shunned and ostracized. But we must persevere in spite of the forces that will be arrayed against us.

> *Many of the male authorities did not then and do not now include the best interests of over half of their population, women and girls, in their legal formulations.*

This will not be a new phenomenon, for Muslim feminists have suffered all manner of abuse in their struggle to achieve women's human rights within Muslim societies. It is the same kind of suffering and abuse experienced by women worldwide as well as racial and religious minorities, slaves, peasants, and workers who have fought for their human rights.

The struggles of Muslim feminists

What is so remarkable about feminist Muslim women's struggles is that their struggle has been waged in largely agrarian societies with high illiteracy rates among men and even more so among women. They are struggling in societies where the hold of religious belief is still great and where religion is an important regulator of everyday life and source of identity. This fact is critical in societies where people are taught that the oppression of women is mandated by their religion. Muslim feminists have had to contend with these deeply held misconceptions about women, which are lodged in their tradition. They have also had to contend with the legacy of the colonialism of the late nineteenth and early twentieth century as well as the American-enforced "New World Order" of today.

Just as in the past, Muslim feminists and their supporters run the risk of being discredited as anti-Islamic, anti-nationalistic, or both. They also run the risk of assassination attempts and legal efforts to change them with apostasy or to have their marriages annulled because they are apostate. Of course this is true for progressive male reformers too. Progressive Muslim scholars such as Farid Esack and Ebrahim Moosa of South Africa have suffered immensely, including assaults on their lives, as a result of their progressive views. Even today a Muslim feminist like Nawal al-Saadawi needs bodyguards when she's at home in Egypt. When Toujan Faisal of Jordan was elected to the lower house of the Jordanian Parliament, she too had to have armed guards to protect her. She was called an apostate; Islamists attempted to have her marriage annulled on the grounds that she was an apostate. They failed in their efforts.

Call to action

We Muslims, feminists, and progressives here in the U.S.A. have the opportunity to practice an Islam that is egalitarian in its precepts and its practices. We must fight to re-interpret the texts in keeping with the socio-historical context of our times. When women are going on space missions and walking on the moon, flying F-16s, performing heart transplants, and so on and so on, can we continue talking and preaching about woman being created from a rib and that this has determined that she is too emotional and mentally fragile to work outside the home or to pursue a meaningful career? The facts on the ground dispute these contentions, resolutely. We must let these myths go. We must bring the best of Islam into the twenty-first century and stop dragging those anti-woman perspectives and interpretations of medieval men into our masjids,[2] our classrooms, our homes, and our hearts.

We have the opportunity to bring about a change. Are we up to the challenge?

2. Muslim places of worship; mosques

Organizations to Contact

The editors have compiled the following list of organizations concerned with the issues debated in this book. The descriptions are derived from materials provided by the organizations. All have publications or information available for interested readers. The list was compiled on the date of publication of the present volume; names, addresses, phone and fax numbers, and e-mail addresses may change. Be aware that many organizations take several weeks or longer to respond to inquiries, so allow as much time as possible.

Federation of Muslim Women
#43093—Mavis Road Postal Outlet, Mississauga, ON L5B 4A7 Canada
(905) 896-7337
e-mail: info@fmw.org • Web site: www.fmw.org

The Federation of Muslim Women is a not-for-profit community-based organization working toward the empowerment of women and children through raising awareness and education that ensures the dignity and worth of all people. Resources include an extensive book list with both adult and children's books on Islam.

Institute for the Secularisation of Islamic Society (ISIS)
e-mail: info@SecularIslam.org • Web site: www.secularislam.org

The Institute for the Secularisation of Islamic Society was formed to promote the ideas of rationalism, secularism, democracy, and human rights within Islamic society. ISIS promotes freedom of expression, freedom of thought and belief, freedom of intellectual and scientific inquiry, freedom of conscience and religion—including the freedom to change one's religion or belief—and freedom from religion: the freedom not to believe in any deity. Publications include articles on the origins of the Koran, an online newsletter, and personal testimonials concerning Islam.

Islamic Circle of North America Sisters' Wing (ICNA)
166-26 Eighty-ninth Ave., Jamaica, NY 11432
(718) 658-1199 • fax: (718) 658-1255
e-mail: info@icna.org • Web site: www.icnasisterswing.org

The Islamic Circle of North America is dedicated to helping establish the Islamic way of life in the lives of Muslims living in North America. A subdivision of ICNA, Sisters' Wing provides women with an opportunity to utilize their skills and work for seeking the pleasure of Allah without intermingling with men. Includes online, downloadable audio files of the Koran.

Islamic Institute for Human Rights (IIHR)
e-mail: info@iifhr.com • Web site: www.iifhr.com

The Islamic Institute for Human Rights is a nonprofit organization dedicated to encouraging a cross-cultural human rights dialogue. IIHR has three core purposes: to promote awareness of the fundamental role of human rights in Islam; to highlight human rights abuses in predominantly Islamic countries (or countries with significant Muslim populations); and to examine specific human rights issues, such as woman's rights, through the lens of Islam. Publications include online articles on honor killings, female genital mutilation, female infanticide, and trafficking of women.

Kamilat
PO Box 391660, Mountain View, CA 94039
(810) 714-3664 • (877) KAMILAT
e-mail: staff@kamilat.org • Web site: www.kamilat.org

Kamilat is a registered nonprofit non-governmental organization that focuses on the social, economic, academic, and spiritual empowerment of women. Publications include women's writings from the hajj (the pilgrimage to Mecca), articles on marriage in Islam, a section on breast cancer and cultural barriers to treatment, and on domestic violence.

Karamah: Muslim Women Lawyers for Human Rights
The T.C. Williams School of Law, University of Richmond
Richmond, VA 23173
(202) 234-7302 • fax: (202) 234-7304
e-mail: karamah@karamah.org • Web site: www.karamah.org

Karamah is a charitable, educational organization that focuses on the domestic and global issues of human rights for Muslims. Its objectives are to increase the familiarity of the Muslim community with Islamic, American, and international laws on the issues of human rights; to advise and assist Muslims, particularly women, on matters that hinder the free exercise of their religion, freedom of expression, and other constitutional rights in the United States; and to provide educational materials on legal and human rights issues to American Muslim women. Online articles include "Laicité (Secularism), Women's Rights, and the Headscarf Ban in France"; "Her Honor: An Islamic Critique of the Rape Laws of Pakistan from a Woman-Sensitive Perspective"; and "Capital Punishment in the United States: An Islamic Perspective."

Muslim Women's League
3010 Wilshire Blvd., Suite 519, Los Angeles, CA 90010
(626) 358-0335
e-mail: mwl@mwlusa.org • Web site: www.mwlusa.org

The Muslim Women's League is a nonprofit Muslim American organization working to implement the values of Islam and thereby reclaim the status of women as free, equal, and vital contributors to society. Its Web site includes articles about gender equity, civil rights, marriage, inheritance, and sexuality.

Revolutionary Association of the Women of Afganistan (RAWA)
PO Box 374, Quetta, Pakistan
0092-300-5541258
e-mail: rawa@rawa.org • Web site: www.rawa.org

The Revolutionary Association of the Women of Afganistan is the oldest political/social organization of Afghan women struggling for peace, freedom, democracy, and woman's rights in Afghanistan. RAWA is an independent political/social organization of Afghan women fighting for human rights and for social justice in Afghanistan. *Afghan Women Challenge the Fundamentalists, The Burst of the "Islamic Government" Bubble in Afghanistan,* and an online photo gallery are available on its Web site.

Sufi Women Organization
14 Commercial Blvd., Suite 101, Novato, CA 94949
(415) 382-7834
e-mail: info@sufiwomen.org • Web site: www.sufiwomen.org

The Sufi Women Organization was established in 1993 under the auspices of the International Association of Sufism. A forum for all Sufi women, it has been tremendously successful in bringing together women from diverse cultural backgrounds who share a dedication to the goals of Sufism, especially with respect to human rights. Publications include a subscription newsletter and online articles on the role of women in religion, women in Islam, and women in the Koran.

United Nations Development Fund for Women (UNIFEM)
Arab States Regional Office
c/o Dr. Haifa Abu Ghazaleh, PO Box 830896, Amman, Jordan 11183
009626-5678-586/7 • fax: 009626-5678-594
e-mail: amman@unifem.org.jo • Web site: www.unifem.org.jo

UNIFEM Arab States Regional Office (ASRO) recognizes the important role of Arab women as central actors in families, communities, and economic and decision-making systems, which necessitates providing them access to essential resources as well as to social services. UNIFEM ASRO believes that the best way to empower Arab women is through strengthening the institutional capacity of the organizations working for and with women, while fostering links and partnerships at the different levels. Publications include *Progress of Arab Women 2004* and *The Status of Jordanian Women: Demography, Economic Participation, Political Participation and Violence.*

Women Living Under Muslim Laws
International Coordination Office
PO Box 28445, London N19 5NZ, UK
e-mail: run@gn.apc.org • Web site: www.wluml.org

Women Living Under Muslim Laws is an international organization that was created to break Muslim women's isolation and to support all women whose lives may be affected by Muslim laws. Its Web publications include articles on empowerment, law reform, state control, sexual/reproductive rights and health, violence against women, sexuality, militarization, and fundamentalism.

Bibliography

Books

Miriam Adeney   *Daughters of Islam: Building Bridges with Muslim Women.* Downers Grove, IL: InterVarsity Press, 2002.

Haleh Afshar   *Islam and Feminisms: An Iranian Case-Study.* Houndmills, UK: Palgrave Macmillan, 1999.

Leila Ahmed   *A Border Passage: From Cairo to America—A Woman's Journey.* New York: Penguin, 2000.

Leila Ahmed   *Women and Gender in Islam: Historical Roots of a Modern Debate.* New Haven, CT: Yale University Press, 1993.

Hamid Algar   *Wahhabism: A Critical Essay.* Oneonta, NY: Islamic, 2002.

Kecia Ali   "Progressive Muslims and Islamic Jurisprudence: The Necessity for Critical Engagement with Marriage and Divorce Law," *Progressive Muslims: On Justice, Gender, and Pluralism,* ed. Omid Safi. Oxford, England: Oneworld, 2003.

Carol Anderson Anway   *Daughters of Another Path: Experiences of American Women Choosing Islam.* Lee's Summit, MO: Yawna, 1995.

Sally Armstrong   *Veiled Threat: The Hidden Power of the Women of Afghanistan.* New York: Four Walls Eight Windows, 2003.

Asma Barlas   *"Believing Women" in Islam: Unreading Patriarchal Interpretations of the Qur'an.* Austin: University of Texas Press, 2002.

Benazir Bhutto   *Daughter of Destiny: An Autobiography.* New York: Simon & Schuster, 1989.

Ergun Mehmet Caner   *Voices Behind the Veil: The World of Islam Through the Eyes of Women.* Grand Rapids, MI: Kregel, 2003.

Miriam Cooke   *Women Claim Islam: Creating Islamic Feminism Through Literature.* New York: Routledge, 2000.

Khaled Abou El Fadl   *Speaking in God's Name: Islamic Law, Authority and Women.* Oxford, England: Oneworld, 2001.

Yvonne Yazbeck Haddad and John L. Esposito   *Islam, Gender and Social Change.* Oxford: Oxford University Press, 1997.

Jennifer Heath	*The Scimitar and the Veil: Extraordinary Women of Islam.* Mahwah, NJ: Hidden Spring, 2004.
Fran Lloyd, ed.	*Contemporary Arab Women's Art: Dialogues of the Present.* London: Women's Art Library, 1999.
Irshad Manji	*The Trouble with Islam: A Muslim's Call for Reform in Her Faith.* New York: St. Martin's, 2004.
Fatima Mernissi and Mary Jo Lakeland	*The Veil and the Male Elite: A Feminist Interpretation of Women's Rights in Islam.* New York: Perseus, 1992.
Hiadeh Moghissi	*Feminism and Islamic Fundamentalism: The Limits of Postmodern Analysis.* London: Zed, 1999.
Azar Nafisi	*Reading Lolita in Tehran: A Memoir in Books.* New York: Random House, 2003.
Anne Sofie Roald	*Islam: The Western Experience.* London: Routledge, 2001.
Omid Safi	*Progressive Muslims: On Justice, Gender, and Pluralism.* Oxford, England: Oneworld, 2003.
Lamia Rustum Shehadeh	*The Idea of Women in Fundamentalist Islam.* Gainesville: University Press of Florida, 2003.
Mohammad Ali Syed	*Position of Women in Islam: A Progressive View.* Albany: State University of New York Press, 2004.
Amina Wadud	*Qur'an and Woman: Rereading the Sacred Text from a Woman's Perspective.* Oxford: Oxford University Press, 1999.
Lynn Welchman, ed.	*Women's Rights and Islamic Family Law: Perspectives on Reform.* London: Zed, 2004.
Michael Wolfe, ed.	*Taking Back Islam: American Muslims Reclaim Their Faith.* New York: Rodale, 2002.

Periodicals

Malek Abisaab and Rula Jurdi Abisaab	"A Century After Qasim Amin: Fictive Kinship and Historical Uses of '*Tahrir al-Mara*,'" *Aljadid*, Winter 2002.
Azhar Abu-Ali and Carol A. Reisen	"Gender Role Identity Among Adolescent Muslim Girls Living in the U.S.," *Current Psychology*, Summer 1999.
Lisa Beyer	"Women and Islam: How Muslim Women Live with the Demands of Their Faith—and Men Who Interpret It," *Time*, December 3, 2001.
Sheryl Henderson Blunt	"Flier Shuns Abaya: Air Force Officer Fights Rule Requiring Her to Wear Muslim Covering," *Christianity Today*, March 11, 2002.

Sarah Childress	"9/11's Hidden Toll: Muslim-American Women Are Quietly Coping with a Tragic Side Effect of the Attacks—a Surge in Domestic Violence," *Newsweek*, August 4, 2003.
Juan R.I. Cole	"The Taliban, Women, and the Hegelian Private Sphere—Part III: Individual, Family, Community, and State," *Social Research*, Fall 2003.
Susan Muaddi Darraj	"Understanding the Other Sister: The Case of Arab Feminism," *Monthly Review*, March 2002.
Hoda Elsadda	"Revisiting Popular Memory and the Construction of Gendered Identity: The Story of a Project," *Middle East Women's Studies Review*, Spring/Summer 2003.
Sarah Eltantawi	"The Politics of Sex," *Minaret*, July 2003.
Haleh Esfandiari	"The Woman Question," *Wilson Quarterly*, Spring 2004.
Zeeshan Hasan	"Islam from Patriarchy to Feminism," *Star Weekend Magazine*, April 14, 1998. www.liberalislam.net/women.html.
Nouha al-Hegelan	"Women in the Arab World," *Rozanehmagazine*, May/June 2003. www.rozanehmagazine.com/MayJune03/womenarab.html.
Kay S. Hymowitz	"Why Feminism Is AWOL on Islam," *City Journal*, Winter 2003.www.city-journal.org.
Pinar Ilkkaracan	"Women, Sexuality, and Social Change in the Middle East and the Maghreb," *Social Research*, Fall 2002.
Farhad Kazemi	"Gender, Islam, and Politics—Iran," *Social Research*, Summer 2000.
Shahrzad Mojab	"Theorizing the Politics of 'Islamic Feminism,'" *Feminist Review*, Autumn 2001.
Caryle Murphy	"Islam & Feminism: Are the Barriers Coming Down?" *Carnegie Reporter*, Fall 2003.
Maryam Namazie	"Islam, Political Islam and Women in the Middle East," *Medusa*, October 2003.
Asra Q. Nomani	"Shaking Up Islam in America," *Time*, September 13, 2004.
Asifa Quraish	"Her Honor: An Islamic Critique of the Rape Laws of Pakistan from a Woman-Sensitive Perspective," *Michigan Journal of International Law*, vol. 18, 1997.
Jen'nan Ghazal Read	"The Sources of Gender Role Attitudes Among Christian and Muslim Arab-American Women," *Sociology of Religion*, Summer 2003.

Madhavi Sunder

"Piercing the Veil. (Women's Human Rights Activists in Muslim Communities)," *Yale Law Journal,* April 2003.

Nayereh Tohidi

"Islamic Feminism: Perils and Promises," *Middle East Women's Studies Review,* Fall 2001/Winter 2002.

Arshia U. Zaidi and Muhammad Shuraydi

"Perceptions of Arranged Marriages by Young Pakistani Muslim Women Living in a Western Society," *Journal of Comparative Family Studies,* Autumn 2002.

Index

125